Forward

I've known Professor Laurie and have been working with his students for nearly ten years. Having known many educators over the years, I've always found Tom to be way ahead of the curve in terms of having a genuine interest in the well-being of his students following their college experience. He has always prided himself on fully understanding the local business market and staying in touch with the attributes (both knowledge and soft skills) of what employers are seeking in new graduates. With this in mind, I fully endorsed the notion of Tom's creating this book and I've enjoyed the finished product.

Unfortunately there haven't been a great deal of quality publications that address the instinctive and intuitive aspects of a job search. The print and web publication world is full of fluff that doesn't resonate with the majority of the interested audience. Have you ever read an article or a book that kept your head nodding in agreement? That is what I found Tom's book did for me. Its simple and concise format cuts to the chase and drives at the important and attainable aspects of career searching, preparation, and execution.

This book is a great preparation tool for a student just entering the employment world as well as a great refresher for someone who has been in the market for some time. I'm looking forward to future publications from Tom.

Jason Alexander
Entrepreneur and Founder of Alexander Technology Group

See More at:

www.TheLosingAttitude.com

Conquer The Losing Attitude of Job Hunters

Step-By-Step Strategies to Search for, Interview for and Secure your Dream Job

Author: Tom Laurie

Attitude Check Press, LLC

271 Narrows Road

Barnstead, NH 03225

2011

To those employers who have had confidence enough to hire me throughout my career

Table of Contents

Introduction

For many years I barely had to look for a job. When I finally did have to look for a job, I was totally unprepared.

Most people I meet have absolutely no idea what it takes to look for and find a job, much less what it takes to be the best candidate for that job. This is not their fault; unfortunately, most parents and schools don't teach these skills.

I believe that the skills you need to successfully find, interview for, and accept the job of your dreams are perhaps the most important skills you will ever learn. It is my goal to teach those skills in this book.

Many times the most qualified person for a job doesn't get the job because someone else makes a better presentation to the company. This is a great shame when it happens, but it doesn't have to happen, because these presentation skills can be learned.

Professor Tom Laurie

Chapter 1: That Downward Spiral?

"It is never too late to be what you might have been."

- George Eliott

JOBLESS

The company I worked for went out of business, and I decided to change careers. I went back to school and updated my degree with a current sought-after certificate and started my job search the only way I knew how (I knew so little back then), by sending out resumes and waiting for the phone to ring.

I have held many exciting careers; aircraft commander, flight instructor, commercial pilot, high school teacher, Information Technology (IT) company CEO, bed and breakfast owner and college professor. I was successful, but I learned more from the jobs I didn't get.

In junior high school, I interviewed for the new McDonald's Restaurant. It was the hot place to work in town, but, you guessed it, I didn't get the job. This was the first job I had ever applied for, and even though I didn't get hired, I walked away with some interviewing experience.

Guess what? Not getting hired for that job didn't affect my chances for getting hired at the next place, unless, I let myself get a *Losing Attitude*. In fact, getting turned down increased my motivation to do better and I was certainly more prepared to answer interview questions the next time. See Answering

Objections, chapter (15) on how to answer questions about experience when you have no or little work experience.

I have been teaching students for many years about what steps they need to take to be successful in their job searches. My classroom is a virtual laboratory where I can instruct students, watch them try different techniques, change my instruction based on their feedback, and end up with a better set of job obtaining techniques and strategies. In this book, I hope you can learn from my mistakes, my students' mistakes, and your mistakes to end up with a step-by-step strategy to search for, interview for and secure your dream job!

After a few false starts, my family and I ended up living in my father-in-law's house, where I began my job search. We had little money and I really needed a job. At this point in my life, I had little job searching experience and I made all the mistakes.

I knew very little about finding and applying for jobs. I used the age old ways of trial and error. You will go through some of this yourself, but I hope that with this book, you can avoid most of the pain.

> On a side note, the town I ended up living in was the town I had declared I would never live in. I started my job search by having to do what I said I would never do -- what a confidence detractor.

I started out spending a few hours updating my resume and got a few hundred copies printed on nice stock at the local print shop. I didn't even think about letting someone critique or proofread my resume. My qualifications were so good that I thought anyone should be happy to hire me. I read the want ads in a couple of local Sunday papers and sent resumes out for the few jobs I thought I qualified for. Then, the waiting game began.

There is nothing more depressing than sitting around the house waiting for a call. When the rejection letters came in, it was even tougher. This vicious cycle of waiting and getting more depressed actually hurt my chances of getting a job. It is this downward spiral, this *Losing Attitude*, that actually makes some people give up hope of finding a job.

I propose that you develop an aggressive hands-on approach to finding a job; this approach will get you out of the house and put you in a position to receive the job you deserve. If you follow the steps in this book, you will have a better chance of finding and then getting a job, whether it is as a pipe fitter or a computer programmer.

> Why did I use this title? In *The Losing Attitude for Dieters* I wanted people to gain that *Losing Attitude* so they could lose weight. In this book, to be successful in finding a job, you must conquer that *Losing Attitude*!

Why People Fail in Their Job Search

- **Losing Attitude.** I have counseled so many job searchers with lousy attitudes. They let the past influence the present. Just because your last job ended badly doesn't mean you can't find a better one -- don't let your past defeats affect your prospects! Just because you got turned down today doesn't mean you won't find a great job tomorrow!

- **Poor Physical Appearance.** As a job searcher, you are in competition with everyone else looking for your job. If you are overweight or you have a lousy haircut or hairstyle or you look like you can't physically handle the job, you are hurting your chances. It is vital that you start working on these areas. You will be amazed at how much the loss of just five pounds will energize you and improve your prospects!

- **Poor Resume.** In a competitive job market, a poor resume can eliminate you from contention on a job you are qualified for. There is no reason why you can't have a compelling resume to best sell yourself! It would be a shame for you and the company that didn't get you, the best qualified person for the job, just because of a poor resume.

- **Poor Cover Letter.** In the rush to apply for a job, many job searchers don't take the time to customize their cover letter for the job they are applying for. A cover letter is the gateway to the job world; many times it is the first chance you have to make a great impression. Don't slack off in this area!

- **Poor Dress.** Jason, a friend of mine who owns a job staffing agency, says that, "No company owner has ever told him that they didn't want to hire his client because the client was overdressed!" Give yourself the best possible chance by dressing properly.

- **Poor Job Search.** Looking for a job is a full-time job -- if you are not spending 30-40 hours a week in your search then you are limiting yourself. Besides, by putting in the time you will not only improve your chances, but will also feel better about yourself.

- **Poor Social Networking.** You must search for a job by all means possible. Many job searchers don't take enough time to ensure their electronic applications are robust and error. Many others fail to use all electronic means necessary. Many have social networking sites that actually hurt their chances of getting a job.

- **Poor Exposure.** Many job hunters limit the areas where they search and limit the type of job they are searching for. Don't shy away from the job staffing agencies. Many times these agencies try to place you in a short-term contract. This may be exactly what you need to jump-start your career and many times these contracts lead to full-time employment.

- **Shyness.** You might not feel great about not having a job and this may cause you not to mention your status to anyone. Don't do it. Many times your friends, family and former associates are the best sources for job leads.

- **Not Working.** A potential employer can be skeptical if they see a candidate who hasn't worked for a long period of time. They might think, "What's wrong with this person since they haven't worked in a year or 2 years?" It is always easier to find a new job when you are working then when you are unemployed.

- **Not Updated.** Are you 10 years behind on the newest technologies in your field because you never thought you would lose your job and, therefore, never bothered to update your skills? If this is true, it is time to go back to school and update your credentials by getting a degree or the latest certificate in your field.

- **Poor Location.** Sometimes you are living in an area where there are very few good jobs in your field. If you are not willing to look in a different location, you are limiting yourself.

- **Poor Research.** How many job hunters show up for an interview without knowing very much about the company they hope to work for? How many job hunters don't even know what they should be paid for their skills? Don't fall behind your competitors by not researching your field.

- **Poor Interviewing Skills.** The interview can be the most important reason you get a job. There is no reason why you should not spend the time to improve your interviewing skills. I have seen many people not get chosen for jobs because of poor interviewing skills -- it doesn't have to be this way.

- **Job Killing Objections.** Many job hunters have something in their past that could be a job killing objection. Some job hunters have something about them that could be seen as a detriment to hiring them. If you are not ready to answer potential objections from a potential employer, then you might fail in your job search.

- **Salary Objections.** Many job hunters don't even apply to places where they don't like the salary. This limits their search; job conditions and advancement opportunities are many times more important than starting salaries. Some companies are just better to work for than others. Do what it takes to get hired into these companies even if it is at a low level. You will be able to move up!

- **No Follow-Up.** Many job hunters don't bother following up with people they meet that might influence their job search. I once interviewed three good candidates for a job and couldn't decide until only one candidate sent me a thank you note for the interview. I hired that candidate!

- **Poor Excitement.** What employer doesn't want to hire someone who is excited about working for them. Many job hunters show little or no excitement for a job even during the interview. This is something you can work on.

> I've probably made errors in each of these areas in my searches for a job -- maybe you have, too! Just because you have made errors doesn't mean you can't turn things around. Get Dynamic, not Depressed!

In the movie "Morning Glory," is a scene where Becky Fuller (Rachel McAdams) interviews for a behind-the-scenes job on a morning TV show. She showed so much enthusiasm and excitement during this interview that I thought that I would have hired her for any job I had, and if I didn't have a job for her, I would have created one.

This is the type of interview you want to shoot for. Although you are probably not a professional actor or actress, you can still aspire to show you are the best person for the job. Imagine if you were so good in your interview that the company didn't hire you for that particular job, but created another job for you!

I have been successfully coaching students for years on the best ways to find a job. Let me help you to improve yourself in these areas so you can be better armed to assault the job market and get the job of your dreams.

Chapter 2: Attitude is Everything

"To different minds, the same world is a hell, and a heaven."

- Ralph Waldo Emerson

Fred Lance, a professor in my department, gives students an extra five points on quizzes if they put "Attitude is Everything" on the top of their papers. He wants to ingrain into their consciousness the idea that attitude is much more important than talent.

He has said many times that he would more willingly recommend a "B-" student with a determined attitude to an employer rather than an "A" student with a lackluster work approach. We talk to many employers and recommend many students for jobs; there are just some who we would never recommend!

COWARD

Desmond T. Doss, because of his religious beliefs, refused to carry a weapon when he enlisted into the Army during World War II. In basic training other enlistees taunted him ruthlessly, threw their boots at him and called him a coward. The Army made him a stretcher carrier.

> Do you let other people define who you are?
>
> The temptation is always there to get down on yourself if you don't get the job you wanted. In reality, you hardly ever know the reason you didn't get hired -- maybe the boss's niece is the one who got the job and the reason you lost the job had nothing to do with you.
>
> Desmond Doss didn't let what other people thought of him affect his actions. He stayed true to his beliefs and lived his beliefs.

MEDAL OF HONOR

Rank and organization: Private First Class, U.S. Army, Medical Detachment, 307th Infantry, 77th Infantry Division. Place and date: Near Urasoe Mura, Okinawa, Ryukyu Islands, 29 April-21 May 1945. Entered service at: Lynchburg, Va. Birth: Lynchburg, Va. G.O. No.: 97, 1 November 1945.

Citation: He was a company aid man when the 1st Battalion assaulted a jagged escarpment 400 feet high. As our troops gained the summit, a heavy concentration of artillery, mortar and machinegun fire crashed into them, inflicting approximately 75 casualties and driving the others back. Pfc. Doss refused to seek cover and remained in the fire-swept area with the many stricken, carrying them 1 by 1 to the edge of the escarpment and there lowering them on a rope-supported litter down the face of a cliff to friendly hands. On 2 May, he exposed himself to heavy rifle and mortar fire in rescuing a wounded man 200 yards forward of the lines on the same escarpment; and 2 days later he treated 4 men who had been cut down while assaulting a strongly defended cave, advancing through a shower of grenades to within 8 yards of enemy forces in a cave's mouth, where he dressed his comrades' wounds before making 4 separate trips under fire to evacuate them to safety. On 5 May, he unhesitatingly braved enemy shelling and small arms fire to assist an artillery officer. He applied bandages, moved his patient to a spot that offered protection from small arms fire and, while artillery and mortar shells fell close by, painstakingly administered plasma. Later that day, when an American was severely wounded by fire from a cave, Pfc. Doss crawled to him where he had fallen 25 feet from the enemy position, rendered aid, and carried him 100 yards to safety while continually exposed to enemy fire. On 21 May, in a night attack on high ground near Shuri, he remained in exposed territory while the rest of his company took cover, fearlessly risking the chance that he would be mistaken for an infiltrating Japanese and giving aid to the injured until he was himself seriously wounded in the legs by the explosion of a grenade. Rather than call another aid man from cover, he

29

cared for his own injuries and waited 5 hours before litter bearers reached him and started carrying him to cover. The trio was caught in an enemy tank attack and Pfc. Doss, seeing a more critically wounded man nearby, crawled off the litter; and directed the bearers to give their first attention to the other man. Awaiting the litter bearers' return, he was again struck, this time suffering a compound fracture of 1 arm. With magnificent fortitude he bound a rifle stock to his shattered arm as a splint and then crawled 300 yards over rough terrain to the aid station. Through his outstanding bravery and unflinching determination in the face of desperately dangerous conditions Pfc. Doss saved the lives of many soldiers. His name became a symbol throughout the 77th Infantry Division for outstanding gallantry far above and beyond the call of duty.

When President Harry S. Truman presented The Congressional Medal of Honor to Desmond Doss, he said, " I'm proud of you, you really deserve this. I consider this a greater honor than being president."

> What are you afraid of? Are you afraid of speaking in public, or maybe you are afraid of meeting new people, or maybe you are afraid of learning new ideas? Everything is possible if you have the right attitude! Start slow, but continue to persevere even if you fail.

CAPTURED

A Colonial woman, Hannah Dustin, her baby daughter Martha, and her nurse Mary were captured in a 1697 raid of Abenaki Native Americans while her husband and eight other children escaped in Haverhill, Massachusetts.

> Do you always make excuses because of the bad things that have happened in your life?
>
> Everyone has bad things happen to them It is not how you are knocked down that defines your life, but how you get up and continue on!

During the trip north, the Native American captors took baby Martha and killed her by slamming her into a tree. The group was later joined by another white captive, 14-year-old Samuel.

When the group stopped on an island in the Merrimack River at the mouth of the Contoocook River at modern day Penacook, New Hampshire, Hannah led a revolt at night with Mary and Samuel after the Native Americans were asleep. They used the Native Americans' own tomahawks to kill 10 of the 12 while a woman and child escaped. They then scalped the dead in order to collect the bounty, used one of their canoes and made their way back to Haverhill, traveling only at night.

In 1879 a bronze statue was placed in Haverhill town square and another on the island in Penacook, New Hampshire. This is possibly the first statue honoring a woman in the United States.

> Although you will probably never be captured in your lifetime, there are all sorts of horrible events that will enter your life. Don't let these events paralyze you; be like Hannah Dustin and take action.

SHORTY

At 6' 9" tall, Bill Russell might have been considered undersized compared to Wilt Chamberlain, the premier big man of his time who towered over Russell at 7' 1". Height certainly matters in basketball, but I believe heart is much more important, as Bill Russell proved again and again during his career.

Bill was the ultimate team player and he had no desire to win the statistical battle -- he just wanted to win the game. He didn't have to play better than Wilt; he just had to make Chamberlain play at a lower level than normal.

> Are there other people that are smarter, faster or more powerful than you?
>
> Don't let your lack of specific abilities stop you from obtaining your goals. A great work ethic and determination has put many people in the hall of fame of life, ahead of other people who possessed greater skills!

Bill wasn't recruited heavily from high school and finally went to the University of San Francisco, whose team had never achieved national success before Russell. He led that team to two NCAA championships in his junior and senior years.

From there he played in the Olympics and helped win the gold medal for the United States in basketball. He was captain of this gold medal team. Bill Russell was so talented that if he hadn't been on the basketball team he probably could have medaled in the high jump.

After the Olympics, Bill Russell joined the Boston Celtics part-way through the season. At this point Boston had never won anything, but through Bill's tremendous will to win, the Celtics won the NBA Championship 11 times out of the next 13 years including that first year; Bill Russell acted as player coach the last two seasons.

Bill Russell was certainly a gifted athlete, but his will to win was legendary. I've heard Tommy Heinsohn, Celtic Hall of Famer, say that Russell had such a desire to win and he was so anxious to win that he threw up before almost every big game. If the team heard Bill throwing up, they knew they would okay that night.

With two NCAA Championships, an Olympic gold medal, and 11 NBA Championships, Bill Russell is, I believe, the Most Valuable Player (MVP) that ever existed in basketball. Bill's attitude was unbelievable and he had to not only overcome other basketball players, but also overcome something much harder.

RACISM

Bill Russell faced an America where racism always seemed to raise its ugly head. In his junior year of college he probably was the best basketball player in the universe, yet he wasn't named Player of the Year in northern California. One time, he and his African-American teammates were not allowed in a hotel in Oklahoma City during a 1954 All College Tournament and had to camp out at a college dorm in the area.

Although his racism problems didn't stop when he went to Boston, I believe that it got better as the years went on. Bill

Russell was on a team that started five African-American players for the first time in NBA history. He was also the first African-American coach in the NBA. In 2010, President Obama awarded Bill Russell the Medal of Freedom -- the highest award allowed for civilians in the United States.

> What kind of problems do you face in your life? Don't let these problems hold you back. Don't let other people hold you back. Use Bill Russell as a model and overcome these problems with your Attitude!

Attitude is everything!

Think about it. Would you want to hire someone who is always complaining about everything or would you rather hire someone who always takes the glass "half full" attitude?

I know that no matter how much attitude I have, I will never be able to dunk a basketball. But, I can be a great teammate if I put the effort into practicing, into playing defense and into studying the plays.

You, too, might have some problems in your life, but you can make yourself a much better employee with the right attitude.

Attitude is everything!

When I ran cross country in high school, we nicknamed our team the "Mudders." If on the way to an away meet, it started raining, we would start to cheer on the bus.

We psyched ourselves up to perform our best in bad weather conditions. I can't remember us ever losing a cross-country race in the rain.

Are you ready for when rain enters your life?

Being positive is a learned habit. You can start right now and see how it will change your life!

Chapter 3: Better Yourself

"Success is something you attract by the person you become."

- Jim Rohn

In the job finding arena, first impressions are many times the difference between getting and losing a job. If you know that, doesn't it make sense to change those things you can so you can make the best first impression possible!

> I have, what you would say is, a great face for radio! There is not much I can do about that, but I can try to make myself better in all the other areas that go into making a good first impression.

As an IT Department Head, I often have job seekers come up to me and ask the question, "If I take your certificate program, will I be able to get a job?" Many times I am looking at a person who is 80 pounds overweight, or is missing teeth, or has long greasy hair or hasn't taken a shower that day and I'm thinking, "Who would ever hire you for any job?"

It is time for you to take a long hard look at yourself in the mirror and...

WEIGHT

Right or wrong, overweight people are discriminated against. Many employers can't see past the perceived medical problems that many overweight people get as they get older.

Many people wrongly associate laziness to someone who is overweight.

This is such an important topic for a job seeker to concentrate on that I have written an entire book on the subject, *The Losing Attitude for Dieters*.

> Should you wait until you have lost the weight you need to lose to look better?
>
> No, you will be amazed at how much better you can look in just the first few days of a diet. Losing those first few pounds usually takes that puffiness out of your face and makes you feel a lot better.
>
> With your newfound energy, you should be ready to get going! Don't let being overweight hold you back from finding your next job. Start dieting and start looking.

SPEECH

Is giving a speech the biggest fear you have in life?

Well, then you are probably going to seem nervous during an interview. Employers expect some nervousness during an interview, but wouldn't a candidate that seemed confident have a little bit of an edge over a nervous candidate?

You can better yourself in the following ways:

- Volunteer to give a speech -- anywhere.
- Find your local chapter of Toastmasters International.
- Join your Rotary Club.
- See if there is some Dale Carnegie training in your area.
- Start teaching a class.
- Get the Dale Carnegie book *How To Win Friends and Influence People.*
- Become a tutor.
- Join the Jaycees.

> I was asked to MC a retirement party for my boss.
>
> It wasn't until just before I had to get up to speak that I realized there were almost 200 people in the audience. Luckily, I had almost finished my meal, as my throat constricted to a size where I could barely swallow some water.

> I'm sure my voice cracked a bit when I started, but I became more and more comfortable the more I talked.
>
> They said I did a great job. Little did they know how terrified I was. Guess what? The next time I had to MC a party, I wasn't nearly as frightened.
>
> All it took was practice. After speaking in front of hundreds of people, I am not in the least bit intimidated about interviews now.

POSITIVE ATTITUDE

You know when you see the type of person who you want to be with; the type of person who seems always happy and upbeat. Don't you want the person who will hire you to think this about you?

I've interviewed a lot of people and many times I interview people who seem to be unhappy or at the best just negative. This is something you can change through practice. I guarantee that if you start acting more positive, you will become a more positive person.

Have a friend interview you and videotape the session. Play it back and see how animated and positive you seem.

Have you ever been watching the local news and some local person is interviewed about what happened and that person looks so wooden and stiff? Now watch the newscasters closely and see what they do with their facial expressions -- watch their eyebrows for a minute.

If you want to seem more positive, more animated, more like the type of person who everyone wants to hire, then start videotaping. Start practicing and videotaping some more.

Only do this if you want the best job possible!

HAIR CUT OR STYLE

Do what it takes to make sure your hair looks good. For a man, your hair needs to look neat and trim. For a woman, you should think about the latest styles.

> If you are a stylishly challenged man like me, then there is hope. Find a girlfriend, a wife or a female relative to help you decide what you need to do.

Put "business hair styles" in your favorite search engine. You will get more photos, tips and videos than you know what to do with. Take the time to find a hair style that is fashionable and that you feel comfortable with.

If you feel better about the way you look, then you will present a more confident self-assured candidate!

Do you want to make a statement with long hair or a beard? Go for it! Just remember that you might lose some jobs because of that statement.

SHYNESS

Are you naturally shy?

This is something you must absolutely work on! I have interviewed people that were so shy I could hardly hear them when they answered my questions. I am sure they must have found a job somewhere, but not with me.

The days of hiring an employee that you can just keep in the back and never let talk to a customer are over. The world is becoming a more connected place every day and you can't afford to be shy.

Force yourself to learn how to be less shy. Maybe you have to join a club or an organization. Maybe you have to just go out and meet new people. Just do what it takes to become less shy. Believe me, it is hard, but it is worth it, because in the end you will be able to meet new people and maybe get your dream job.

I was so shy with members of the opposite sex that it took me a week to get up the courage to ask my future wife out on a date. I'm sure that there are not too many people out there that were as shy as I was in this area. If I could become less shy than anyone can!

Chapter 4: The Cover Letter

"A cover letter is your opportunity to make a compelling case for yourself as a candidate, totally aside from what's in your resume. That because for most jobs, picking the best candidate is rarely solely about skills and experience. Those obviously take center stage, but if that's all that mattered, there would be no point in interviews; employers would make a hire based off of resumes alone. But in the real world, other factors matter too—people skills, intellect, communication abilities, enthusiasm for the job, and simply what kind of person you are. A good cover letter effectively conveys those qualities."

- Alison Green

PURPOSE

What is the purpose of your cover letter? Are you sending your resume to a company to apply for a specific job or are you sending your resume to inquire about a possible position?

The advantage of the cover letter is that you can customize it to be very specific to the job you are applying for, the company you are applying to, and the skills that are most appropriate to this job. You can certainly customize your resume, but not as easily as you can customize your cover letter.

> In a cover letter you bring to light areas of your life that make you the perfect fit for a specific company or job. I've seen job hunters tell a story about a certain event in their life that would be out of place on a resume, but totally appropriate on a cover letter.

Rarely are people hired based solely on their technical skills. In this day and age, employees are expected to interact with customers on a daily basis. A cover letter is a great way to show off your writing skills. If writing is not your best skill, then you can show off your determination, by getting a lot of help writing the perfect cover letter.

A great cover letter complements your resume and allows you to highlight areas where you would be a great fit for a particular job. You do this by spending the time needed to create a compelling cover letter by adding your personal touch.

Many job hunters get so excited about a potential job that they rush the cover letter process. In a competitive job market, a gripping cover letter might be the difference between getting an interview or not.

The best way to create your cover letter is to just start writing. If you write too much, then it is easy to keep the best stuff. The items below can be included in your cover letter.

ITEMS TO INCLUDE

- **Contact Information** - Make sure the employer is able to contact you for an interview.
- **Sales Pitch** - You should spend the most time creating your opening paragraph. You need to entice the employer to read the rest of the cover letter. This paragraph is the hook that makes you an interesting candidate. You may want to write this paragraph last.
- **What Job** - Be very specific as to what job you are applying for. Larger companies may have hundreds of

jobs open and you want to make sure your resume gets to the right place.

- **Why Are you Writing?** - Why do you want this job? If there is something about this job or company that excites you, then this is the time to mention it.

- **How Did You Learn?** - Include how you found out about this job, especially if you were referred by a colleague.

- **Quotes** - If you have a favorite quote that just describes the essence of your being, then you might want to include it in your cover letter. Some people feel that a great quote is the perfect way to wrap up your cover letter.

- **What Qualifies Candidate?** - Here is a chance to give a short bulleted list of what qualifies you best for the job. This list differs from similar lists in your resume in that each bulleted point should refer to a quality asked for in the job advertisement.

- **Reflect Your Attitude** - What motivation and enthusiasm will you bring to the job. Employers want to hire people that are excited about the job and the company. Figure out a way to show excitement.

- **Invitation to Resume** - Invite the employer to see your resume for more examples and more detail.

- **Specifically Requested Information** - Many times the job application will ask for information, like your availability to start work, that is not in your resume.

- **Match Skills and Experience** - Here is a chance to rephrase, if needed, your skills and experience so that they match what was advertised exactly. Let's say that your resume highlights a GM automotive diagnostic analysis skill and the shop you are applying at has a different name for this skill. You would want to highlight this difference in your cover letter.

- **Salary Requirements** - Many companies want to know your salary requirements right away. The cover letter is a great place to start.

- **Call to Action** - You never get anything in life unless you ask for it. Make sure you ask to be interviewed for this job.

I've tried to include a mixture of cover letters in APPENDIX A. Remember, your resume is a generic advertisement for yourself; a cover letter allows you to personalize your qualities and skills for a specific job.

The cover letter is one of the first steps to getting your dream job. Take the time to write, edit and proofread your cover letter. There are unlimited resources on the web where you can get ideas for a better cover letter. Don't forget to ask

your friends and family for help in develo₁
cover letter.

Chapter 5: The Resume

"Boxing was the only career where I wouldn't have to start out at the bottom. I had a good resume."

- Sugar Ray Leonard

your friends and family for help in developing your winning cover letter.

Chapter 5: The Resume

"Boxing was the only career where I wouldn't have to start out at the bottom. I had a good resume."

- Sugar Ray Leonard

A well-written resume is worth its weight in gold when it comes to making a marketable presentation of your skills and worth to a potential company. A compelling resume won't guarantee a job, but a poorly written one can be the kiss of death when it comes to getting an interview!

OBJECTIVES

Skill Presentation - In the candidate selection process, many times a resume is not read thoroughly, but scanned for key words which are applied to a skills matrix to make the first cut.

Think about it. You are a hiring manager who just received 500 resumes for the job you just posted. You want the best person for the job, but you don't have the time to scrutinize 500 resumes. You give your secretary a list of key skills and ask her to return to you only the resumes that contain them.

Place your skills in the top third of your resume if possible to make it easy for this skills sift. Be sure to go over a job announcement with a fine-tooth comb and make sure that any skills mentioned are on your resume. What a shame it would be if you gave a skill a different name than the job you wanted did and you never got invited for an interview.

What do you do if a job lists a skill that you don't have? Well, you could research that skill and then put in a section on your resume titled "Skills I am Familiar with."

Bonding - A resume is a great way to present compelling stories about yourself. I have read resumes that made me think the person was so interesting that I couldn't wait to meet them at the interview.

Spend a lot of time on your work experience. Through the use of action words and persuasive narratives, I have seen resumes where a person is described as performing in the most wonderful job in the world where on other resumes the same job might be thought of as a common dull job. This might be a great place to get a professional writer to help.

Experience - You need to list your work experience on a resume. To qualify for some jobs, the employer must be able to easily determine how many years of experience you have in a certain area. To do this, you must place the dates you were employed in these jobs.

I have a running debate with my friend Jason who owns a staffing agency. I say that there is age discrimination out there and he is adamant that you must put as much detail into a resume as you can.

When I tried to get my first job in the
Information Technology field after many years of
being a pilot, I sent out a standard resume with all
my years of employment and the year I graduated
from college. In a little over a year of searching, I
never got one IT interview. I always felt that they
looked down at the bottom of the resume and
said, "Old guy."

I spent the next three years teaching high school
and running the school's computer lab; when I
ventured back into the job market, I sanitized my
resume so that you really couldn't tell how old I
was. I realize that at this time I had more IT
experience and the market had changed, but I got
seven interviews in the first month. I don't think
I will ever believe that I wasn't a victim of age
discrimination the first time around.

The beauty of the electronic age is that you can have several
different resumes. If you feel that you might have a problem
because of your age, then send out some resumes where you
can't tell how old you are and send out some resumes that tell
everything and see what happens.

If you are going through a staffing agency, I suggest that your resume has every possible detail about yourself that you can think of. This is because with a staffing agency you have an advocate giving your resume to an employer. A good agent can take age right off the table by saying something like, "You might never have a candidate with this much experience!"

Advertise Yourself - The resume is not the time to be shy about yourself. Let's face it, in order to get the job, you have to sell yourself.

Don't hesitate to emphasize your strengths. Take the time to craft your descriptions. For instance, you could describe your work at the front counter of a fast-food restaurant in the following two ways. Which do you think is best?

Served customers on a daily basis in my front counter position.

or ...

Continually worked with customers to make their fast food experience memorable; front line solution to customer problems.

TIPS

Brevity - Here is another area where it differs whether or not you are going through a staffing agency or not. If you are sending out resumes to jobs you have seen on-line or in the newspaper, then if you can, I would try to keep your resume down to one page. This is because many hiring managers have full-time responsibilities of their own and the idea of slugging through a seven-page resume might seem daunting to them. Your resume may go unread, especially if there are many applications for a job.

Again, if you are going through a staffing agency, then I would fill your resume with as many details as you can. Don't just fill up the pages to fill up the pages, but if you have a pertinent detail, make sure it is on your resume.

If you got an interview using a one pager, you might consider bringing several copies of a more detailed resume with you to hand out at the interview. This way, your one-page resume got you the job and once they are interested in you, they are more willing to read every detail of your life.

Skills vs. Knowledge - There is a big difference from having taken a one-week crash course on a subject and having worked in that area on a daily basis for years. You certainly want to mention your familiarity with that subject if you took that course, but you don't want to be asked questions you would only be able to answer if you had an in-depth knowledge of the subject. Just be clear in your resume between the difference of a knowledge (familiarity) and a skill.

Objective - Most experts will be divided on whether you should have an objective or not. I have found that in most cases, I don't want to waste valuable resume real estate by putting in an objective; especially if I am trying to keep my resume down to one page. All experts will agree that if you do use an objective, it should be customized for the company you are applying at.

Name - Obviously, you need to have your name on the resume. You don't need to have your name screaming out in billboard size letters. I would rather keep my name and address down to one or two lines and save the extra space for my skills and experience.

Spelling and Grammar - How silly is it to give the person hiring you the idea that either you can't spell or you didn't care enough about the job that you didn't have someone proofread your resume. Take the time, spend the money, and ask the right questions to get a resume that is free of errors.

Active Voice - Use and active voice when describing your experiences. Instead of saying, "The six person advance team was effectively managed," you should say, "Effectively managed six person advance team."

Customize - Take the time to customize your resume to the job you are applying for. Move your skills around, add skills or change the wording of skills so that they better match the skills advertised. Be very careful not to introduce spelling and grammatical errors.

No Pronouns - Instead of saying, "I completed all required courses in record time," you should say , "Completed all required courses in record time."

No Pictures or Fancy Paper - If you think that turning your resume in on purple paper or with a beautiful color picture of yourself will make your resume stand out, you are correct. It will make it easier to eliminate. Possibly, if you are applying for a job such as a graphic artist, you can take some liberties and show your creativity, but normally it is not a good idea. Use your creativity to weave some wonderfully persuasive stories about your experiences.

Don't Waste Space - Don't bother putting in lines like "References available on request" or "Available for interview." Is there anyone out there that doesn't have references or isn't available for an interview?

Use Bullets - The content of a resume is most important, but the entire visual look of the resume gives the first impression. By using bulleted items, you can highlight skills in a way that draws attention to them. In their book *Expert Resumes for Computer and Web Jobs*, Wendy Enelow and Louise Kursmark recommend using a combination format when they are describing an experience by starting with a paragraph followed by bullets. See APPENDIX B for many resume examples using this style.

Weave a Story - To get hired, you must form a connection between yourself and the interviewer. Spend the time when writing your experiences in your resume to weave a story that will help form this connection. Just like a movie trailer, these stories should make the reader want to know more about you.

Chapter 6: Aerobic Job Search

"Do you want to know who you are? Don't ask. Act! Action will delineate and define you."

- Thomas Jefferson

GET OUT

Do not sit at home waiting for the job to come to you!

It doesn't do you any good to just sit there. It can actually do you harm if you just sit there feeling sorry for yourself; believe me, I've been there.

The aerobic approach to finding a job consists of two major themes: First, you must tell everyone that you know and meet that you are looking for a job and second, you must go out to as many potential job sites that you can every day and spread the word.

TELL EVERYONE

Every multi-level marketing company always tells their new recruits to sit down and make a list of all their friends and family; these will be the first set of people these new recruits go to at the beginning of their marketing. The reason they suggest this strategy is because it works.

I suggest the same strategy. Make a list of all your friends and relatives and call each and every one of them and tell them you are looking for a job and what type of job you are looking for.

You might not think that your Aunt Myrtle knows about any

job opportunities, but you might be surprised. Many times your friends and relatives can give you a hot tip on a job they just heard about. Many of my students have received leads from their relatives that have led to internships and eventually great jobs.

If you have an annoying Uncle Bob (or you fill in the name), be sure to tell him because he will probably tell 100 people about the nice young niece or nephew who is looking for a job. Maybe Uncle Bob will even pass out some resumes?

PASS OUT BUSINESS CARDS

Go to your local print shop and have them help you design and print a few hundred business cards that have your contact information and the idea that you are looking for a job. You can usually have these printed up quite inexpensively.

---

603 555-1212
jseeker@yahoo.com

Job A. Seeker
"I'm looking for an entry level job in
<fill in industry> and I'm willing to
start at the bottom and work my way
up!"

Always carry a bunch of these with you and hand them out to everyone you meet. Don't discriminate by thinking a person might not be able to help you. You never know when the little old lady behind you at the convenience store has a son that owns a company in the field you want to work in.

> My wife and I were going to the Highland Games for the first time. I had 60 dollars in my wallet, thinking that Scotts were renowned for being thrifty, surely, that would be enough.
>
> After we bought our tickets and went through the gate, we headed straight for the ATM, as my wallet had been cleaned out.
>
> While waiting at the ATM, I struck up a conversation with the man behind me in line. It turns out that he owned an IT company and was looking for interns. This ended up being a great contact for me, and one of my students ended up getting an internship at his company! Had I been shy, this opportunity would never have presented itself.

Learn how to meet people, give them your card and tell them you are looking for a job. If you are shy, then you need to find a way to get over it because finding and securing a job is a people skill that you need to develop and you just can't afford to be shy.

CATALOGUING YOUR FIELD

Every night you need to make a list of companies in your area that employ people in your field. Go on-line if you can and search using your city and state and key words from your field. Try to group these companies by area.

Every morning, get up, put on your business clothes, grab a stack of cover letters and resumes, and get out of your house. Start by visiting the first business on your list. Make sure you have a notebook or an electronic way to write down information about each company you visit.

Your goal at each company is to find out who hires people in your field at that particular place, leave a cover letter and resume for that person and try to meet them if you can. When you walk into a company, you need to say,

> "Hello, my name is <your name>. Would you please tell me who in your company hires <job name> people?"

The key here is not to ask a question that can be answered with a simple yes or no. The easiest way to get rid of someone asking questions is to just say no!

On the other hand, if you ask who hires the people in your field, then they just can't say no. At this point you need to ask a few more questions (let's say the person who hires is Mr. Apple) and record the answers. You then need to ask:

> "Is Mr. Apple in Human Resources or is he in the <job name> department?"

> "May I get Mr. Apple's contact information? Do you have one of his business cards?"

> "I'm looking for a job in <job name>. Would it be possible to talk to Mr. Apple?"

If they don't let you talk to Mr. Apple (probably most of the time this will be the case), then you ask,

> "May I leave my resume and cover letter for Mr. Apple? I would like to follow up with him in a few days."

At the very least, you should come away from these companies with the name and contact information of the hiring manager in your field. Sometimes you actually get to meet the hiring manager, and, if you are lucky, they might even have a job for you!

> Why are we taking this approach? Most of these companies probably aren't even hiring right now.

You are building a catalog of all the companies and hiring managers in your field in your area. Your goal is to periodically follow up with these managers and hope your name will become familiar to them.

Believe me, when a manager loses an employee, the last thing the manager wants to do is go through the long and drawn out process of advertising, searching through resumes, interviewing, and then hiring a person. If your resume is still sitting on this manager's desk, how easy is it for the manager to pick up the phone and call you!

The key to this strategy is to compete for the jobs before the company goes through the exhausting job hiring process. Wouldn't it be better to compete against a handful of candidates rather than hundreds of them?

Once you leave the company you just visited, be sure to document the information you found out. A day or two later you follow up by calling the company and asking for the hiring manager by name. Amazingly, the same receptionists or secretaries that stonewalled you when you visited the company will put your call through without a moment's hesitation when you call asking for the hiring manager.

When you get through to the hiring manager, you might say something like,

> "Mr. Apple, this is <your name>, Is this a convenient time to talk or should I call at another time?"

If the hiring manager says it is a bad time then ask when would be a better time. If it is a good time then you might say something like,

> "I visited your company a few days ago and left a cover letter and resume for you. May I ask you a few questions about your company?"

The key here is that you should never ask if they have a job for you. That type of question is too direct and never creates the right type of atmosphere.

When I owned a real estate agency and we sold a property in a neighborhood, we would always call the neighbors up and down the street to tell them about their new neighbors.

Our goal here was not only to be portrayed as professional real estate agents, but to generate new leads.

We would say something like, "Hello, this is Mr. Realtor from Friendly Realty and we would like to tell you about your new neighbors who have just purchased Mr. So And So's property at 123 Any Street.

After we had told them about their new neighbors, we would say something like, "Our advertising for 123 Any Street has generated such excitement about your neighborhood, so we were wondering if you knew of any of your neighbors were thinking of selling?"

This is a totally non-threatening way to ask this question. Of course, you are really hoping they will say, "Well, I don't know about any of our neighbors, but we have been thinking of selling."

In the same way, as you are talking to the hiring manager, you should ask,

> "Do you know of any of your colleagues who are hiring any <job name> workers right now?"

Again, this is a totally nonthreatening way of asking this question. Of course, you are hoping the hiring manager will say, "I don't know about them, but we just had an opening come up. When can we meet?" If this doesn't happen, sometimes the hiring manager can give you a couple of leads. If nothing else, your name will undoubtedly become more familiar to this manager.

Make sure you document these conversations. You are building a catalog of names that you will e-mail or call every so often. In your e-mails, you can mention an article you just read about your field or a book you just read in your field or a new updated certificate you just received. Always mention you are still searching for just the right job and ask if the hiring manager has heard of any openings in other companies.

This catalog is worth its weight in gold. After you get your job, be sure to keep in contact with these hiring managers, as you never know when you will need a new job.

> I remember reading a story about a man who left his secure state job to go work for a high-tech company during the height of the dot com boom.
>
> He started his job on a Monday and on Friday all the employees received their pink slips. I hope he still had his catalog of hiring managers!

You might be thinking, wow, this sounds like a lot of work. You are right, but nothing in this world is easy and the rewards for finding your dream job are incalculable. I know you will feel so much better about yourself if you are getting out of your house every day and being productive.

APPLICATIONS

What if you are in an industry that requires you to fill out an application at a company? I would thank them and take the application to fill out at home. Make sure you still try to get the hiring manager's contact information.

How many times have you seen a young person slouching at a counter at one of these companies trying to fill out an application? You can just imagine the misspellings, poor grammar, poor penmanship, and inaccurate data on that application not to mention the first impression the poor posture is creating. Make this application count -- take it home and fill it out correctly!

At home be sure to spend a lot of time filling out the application with the best information you can come up with. My handwriting is just this side of terrible, so I always try to find a way to type applications or get someone with great handwriting to help me.

The next day, you can deliver your application along with your resume and cover letter and hope they make you stand out. A call or e-mail to the hiring manager after a couple of days will certainly help out also!

Chapter 7: Dress for Success

"You cannot climb the ladder of success dressed in the costume of failure."

- Zig Ziglar

IMPACT

Wouldn't it be nice if you could show up for an interview in your jeans and T-shirt and the interviewer just looked at you as a person and saw straight through to your talent? It's a nice dream, but in reality, you are judged immediately when you show up for an interview by what you are wearing. How many times will the person designated to find the best person for their company be thinking, "How could I ever let this person represent my company dressed in that way?"

Brand-new Air Force 2nd Lieutenants or "butter bars" as they are sometimes called don't command a lot of respect. Many enlisted troops will actually try to look the other way rather than having to salute one. It doesn't get any better as a 1st Lieutenant when the bar turns from bronze to silver -- "Sorry, sir, I thought you were a 2nd Lieutenant!"

I remember the day I made Captain. I put on my fancy dress uniform with my silver wings, my medals and my new Captain's rank and went to have my official photo taken.

As I was driving down the road, an Airman stopped on the side of the road and saluted me while I was still in my car. I was so taken aback that I almost botched the return salute.

It was on that day that I realized what an impact you could have on people by the way you dressed!

MOTIVATION

Have you ever heard the old quote, "Dress for the job you want, not the job you have?" Dressing better may not only have an effect on other people, but on you, as well. Most people don't realize how the people in positions above them, whether their teachers or bosses, have a great ability to affect their lives.

I had a student in high school that always wore button-down shirts when every other guy in school looked like they got their clothes from the bottom of their laundry bins. Even though he received some grief from his classmates, I always felt that he carried himself with much more poise and maturity than the other students.

When the time came for college applications, he got the best recommendations from his teachers. In the end, he got a full scholarship to the college of his choice. Not only did his dress have an meaningful effect on his teachers, but I'm sure it helped with his confidence and self-esteem.

FIRST IMPRESSION

Whenever I conduct an interview I immediately categorize every interviewee when that person walks into the room. I don't intentionally do this; it is a subconscious habit.

If a person comes in looking sloppy or is inappropriately dressed, then they have an uphill battle during the interview to overcome this first impression. Wouldn't it be better if you came into the interview being the sharpest looking person there that day?

INTERVIEW CLOTHES

You don't have to have multiple interview outfits. All you have to have is one nice one.

Sometimes financial concerns make it hard to have a great interview outfit. If this is true, then you have to be a little more creative in finding your clothes. I have seen people find some pretty striking outfits at places like Goodwill or the Salvation Army.

> When I was interviewing for a commercial pilot position, it was essential to show up looking sharp and confident. I spent a lot of money on a great looking suit and am glad I did.
>
> The interview for Pan American World Airways lasted a week. In a thorough interview like this, you can believe that they took a good look at how you looked in a suit and whether or not you fit the professional pilot image.

STATEMENT CLOTHES

You must dress appropriately for the job you are trying to get. If you want to dress with a flair, then it might be okay if you are applying for an acting job or a job as an artist. It might not be appropriate if you are applying to be a bank teller.

CLOTHES MAKE THE MAN/WOMAN

Mark Twain had a great quote about this, "Clothes make the man. Naked people have little or no influence on society."

Are clothes really that important?

I don't like to wear a tie and never have, but there are times when I need to wear a suit to school. I must admit that on days I wear my suit, people look at me differently than on days I don't. When I am wearing the suit, people that would hardly ever look my way all of a sudden say, "Hello!"

Take the time to look good when you are coming in contact with potential employers. It is worth it!

Chapter 8: On-line Job Sites

" The discipline of writing something down is the first step toward making it happen."

- Lee Iacocca

JOB SEARCH SITES

There is a wealth of information on many job search sites and a wealth of services. To me, the most valuable services provided by these sites are:

- **Job Search** - By submitting key words from your resume and a desired location, you can come up with a list of current available jobs. Remember, if you choose to apply for these jobs, you are now competing with hundreds, if not thousands, of other applicants.

- **Company Search** - If you are following the aerobic approach of job finding outlined in chapter 6, then these sites are a great way to find companies that you want to visit. Just as above, enter key words from your resume and a location to find companies that are currently offering jobs in your field.

- **Resume Posting** - Here is a way to post your resume where an employer can find it by searching with their defined criteria.

- **Knowledge** - These sites not only have volumes of articles on resumes, cover letters, career planning and the like, but they also many times have message board communities where you can ask questions and get answers.

So, which site is the best?

That's easy. The site where you find your dream job is the best!

Here is a list of some job sites in no particular order:

- **Monster.com** - Definitely the most advertised and thus the most well-known of all the job search sites
  - o **Job Search** - Very easy and understandable search. Gives full information on jobs and allows you to apply right there.
  - o **Company Search** - Excellent way to collect company names.
  - o **Resume Posting** - Allows you to upload your resume or to cut and paste your resume.
  - o **Knowledge** - Extensive data on creating your resume and cover letters, career planning and many community message boards.
- **CraigsList.org** - This is the place to search if you are looking for volume.
  - o **Job Search** - You might not like the categories you can choose from, but you will never be unhappy with the speed of the site. You usually apply through a CraigsList e-mail that is forwarded to the employer.

- o **Company Search** - Almost impossible to find companies' names.
- **CareerBuilder.com** - Claims to be the U.S.'s largest on-line job site. More than 23 million unique visitors come to the website every month.
  - o **Job Search** - Job search was very easy and fast. You can apply right on-line by uploading your resume and cover letter. You can even get a resume critique on the spot when you apply.
  - o **Company Search** - Great way to build your company list.
  - o **Resume Posting** - Allows you to upload your resume or to cut and paste your resume.
  - o **Knowledge** - Full range of advice and resources. I particularly liked the Salary Calculator where you can compare a proposed or current salary against national averages.
- **Indeed.com** - Claims to be the number one worldwide jobsite with more than 50 million unique visitors every month.
  - o **Job Search** - Simple job search. I wanted to be more specific.
  - o **Company Search** - Okay way to build your company list.
  - o **Resume Posting** - Requires you to set up an account to apply for a job.

- o **Knowledge** - Had a nice salary comparison by location, an interesting trends section, and many relevant forums.
- **USAJOBS.com** - USAJOBS is the U.S. Government's official system/program for Federal jobs and employment information. USAJOBS delivers a service by which Federal agencies meet their legal obligation (5 USC 3327 and 5 USC 3330) providing public notice of Federal employment opportunities to Federal employees and U.S. citizens.
  - o **Job Search** - Simple job search with better location than key word results.
  - o **Company Search** - Not great due to the lengthy application process of most government jobs.
  - o **Resume Posting** - As you can imagine, the government gives you great detail on how to apply for these positions.
  - o **Knowledge** - Extensive knowledge base for specific areas like Veterans or recent grads.
- **LinkedIn.com** - World's largest professional network website in the world. You must be a member to access job searches.
  - o **Job Search** - Great job search for professionals.

- o **Company Search** - Good way to build your professional company list. If this is not your first job, then I hope you have used LinkedIn to build your industry contact list.
- o **Resume Posting** - Can apply directly on-line to open positions.
- o **Knowledge** - Nice learning center to find out how to use LinkedIn to its maximum potential.

On-line Job Sites are a great way to give you maximum exposure to the job world. They are also a great way for you to do research on your particular field. Also, you can work on these sites at night or during the weekend when you can't visit companies.

Don't fall into the trap of relying totally on on-line job sites. Face-to-face networking is always the best way to find a job. Use these on-line sites for what they are best at. You should spend, at most, 20% of your time on these sites.

Be aware that once you post a resume on one of these sites, you are opening yourself up for a number of scams and a number of unwanted advertisements.

You will never have to jump through any unnecessary hoops or be asked to give money upfront for a legitimate job. Beware!

LINKEDIN

LinkedIn is a fantastic way to keep in touch with your colleagues while you have a job. This site allows you to watch your colleagues' job progression and allows you to update them on yours.

You can keep everyone abreast of your projects by making updates to your profile. If you need to find a job, you can change your status and the word will get out fast. If you have kept up a relationship with your colleagues through LinkedIn, you might be able to find a new job easily.

FACEBOOK

Employers are getting more sophisticated every day when it comes to Facebook and other on-line social networks. They will use every means available to research the person they plan on hiring.

Think about it from an employer's point of view. They are scared to death that the person they hired, who interviewed incredibly well, will turn into the employee from hell. To keep this from happening, they will try to find out as much information about an employee as possible.

I went to a seminar on Facebook security given by a female police officer who claimed she had over twenty different Facebook aliases. Many of these accounts had pictures of some great looking individuals, both male and female.

She started out the lecture by listing the students on my campus who she had friended. I recognized one of my students and in class the next day I asked him if he had friended a girl named Amber. He said he had and I mentioned that she was not really Amber, but a police officer. His hands practically flew as he logged in to unfriend her.

I know that you probably feel comfortable that you have all your Facebook settings secure and nobody can see anything on your page that you don't want them to see. Well, that might not be exactly correct:

- Facebook changes the permission settings frequently and you might expose some private areas of your page before you know of the changes
- You might friend someone who isn't who they say they are

- You may have all your security settings tight as a drum, but your friends might not. If an employer sees that many of your friends have questionable character, it doesn't reflect well on you.

I would suggest that you create two Facebook accounts. Create one that has no connection to your name (use an alias) and use this account with all your friends. Create another account that is your professional account and is associated with your name. Make sure you don't put anything on this account that you wouldn't share with your future employer.

Chapter 9: Job Staffing Agencies

"Energy and persistence conquer all things."

- Benjamin Franklin

A LITTLE HELP FROM YOUR FRIENDS

When seeking your dream job, it is important that you explore all possible avenues. You need to network with your friends, relatives and associates; you need to get out and network with as many companies in your field as you can; you need to establish your electronic presence on the net, and you need to sign up with a job staffing agency.

There are many advantages to aligning yourself with a job staffing agency. These agencies work for and are paid by companies looking to fill a position. Many loyal companies trust them to find the perfect fit for a job. As the staffing agencies want to keep a great relationship with these companies, they won't recommend you if they don't think you are a good fit. If they think you would a great asset, they'll highly recommend you to a company. This can lead to your working on a contract basis with an employer, which often leads to a full-time job.

PROFESSIONAL JOB COUNSELORS

The counselors that work with you at these staffing agencies are experts in helping you develop a strategic plan for your career. Not only will they help you find your next job, but they will monitor your career and suggest when it is best for you to move on and search for a new job with more responsibilities and better pay.

They will evaluate your work experience and help you formulate a plan for seeking your dream job. They may be brutally honest with you and set up a plan for you to follow so you will be competitive. This plan will highlight the areas that you need to improve, whether it be losing weight, dressing better, interviewing better, or having a better resume. Sometimes they will recommend that you go back to school to improve your skills.

RESUMES

When you are working with a staffing agency, you will be counseled to make your resume as complete as possible. You don't have to worry about the length or about giving away your age.

When your resume is presented to a company by a staffing agency, you have an advocate presenting your skills. You don't need to worry if it takes four pages to accurately describe your skills and experiences because when the company is only looking at one resume, they will take the time to read all of it.

Age on a resume is not a factor when working with a staffing agency, because, again, you have an advocate presenting your resume. I have a friend at a staffing agency that once placed a 81-year old man in a job!

INTERVIEWING

Usually, you will start out your relationship with a job staffing agency by interviewing with them. This is a great opportunity for you to practice your skills and to receive constructive criticism.

You have an advantage when a staffing agency sends you out to a company for an interview. If this company has established a relationship with the staffing agency, they are already expecting a compatible candidate.

This does not lessen your responsibility to interview well. You must do all the company research and interview practice needed to shine during the interview. Don't lose the advantage you have by showing up unprepared.

CAREER PROGRESS GUIDANCE

Don't look for a job without taking advantage of a job staffing agency. Let them help you develop your career strategic plan and let them guide your progress. Wouldn't it be great to get a call from the staffing agency telling you that they have the perfect upgrade job for you?

Chapter 10: Friends, Family and Associates

"It's the friends you can call up at 4 a.m. that matter."

- Marlene Dietrich

SOCIAL ENGINEERING

Kevin Mitnick was a genius at social engineering. He was able to penetrate some of the most secure computer systems in this country by exploiting human nature. People just wanted to help him out and they unknowingly let him hack into their secure networks.

I believe that it is human nature to want to help other people. It is extraordinary how far some people will actually go to help a friend or relative!

EGO

I watched the movie, *The Company Men*, the other night, and I found it intriguing how many of the laid off workers in the movie went to great lengths not to let their friends, families and associates know they had lost their jobs. I kept thinking that someone might have the perfect lead to a great job, but the unemployed person would never find out about it. The person's ego kept him from telling everyone he was looking for a job.

Losing a job is hard. Swallow your ego and tell everyone that you are now on the market. You will find that it is not as bad as you thought and you will find that some of these people can be a valuable resource in finding your next job.

FAMILY

Your family can be a valuable resource. Don't disqualify any of them because you don't think they can help you in your search.

> If I had a dollar for every student that found an internship through a family contact, I'd be able to retire. I remember one student telling the class that he didn't bother telling his parents that he was looking for an internship because he didn't think they knew anyone in the IT field.
>
> As a last resort he asked his mother and she immediately told the student about a neighbor who worked in the IT field. This particular student ended up getting a great internship at that company that led to a job after graduation, all because of his mother!

Take the time to contact all of your relatives. Tell them that you are now looking for a job and tell them specifically what type of job you are looking for. Ask them if they might have any leads.

If you printed up the cards described in chapter 6, then ask each relative if they would be willing to hand out any for you.

Your family might even be willing to hand out resumes for you.

FRIENDS

Your friends are a great pool of knowledge that will be more than willing to help you in your job search. They probably know already that you are looking for a job, so all you have to do is ask for their help.

Have your friends read your resumes and cover letters and help you refine them until they are perfect. Then give your friends electronic copies and ask them to distribute them freely.

> When Pan American World Airways went out of business, there were a lot of us looking for pilot jobs all at once. I tried to keep in touch with my friends from Pan Am as well as I could.
>
> I was sitting in my house one day waiting for the phone to ring with a job offer, and it did. It wasn't any of the airlines I had applied to, but it was one of my friends from Pan Am, who had just gotten a job as chief pilot for a small airline and was calling to offer me a job.

ASSOCIATES

Your former associates know your industry well and can provide some of the best leads. If you have done your job of developing a network of associates in your field, then they are the first people you want to let know that you are looking for a new job.

Chapter 11: BETTER TO BE WORKING

"If you don't want to work you have to work to earn enough
money so that you won't have to work."

- Ogden Nash

CHRONICALLY UNEMPLOYED

If I am interviewing someone and I see that they have not worked for a couple of years (other than taking a break to raise children), I am immediately skeptical of this person. I keep thinking, "What is it about this person that has kept them from getting a job for so long? Do they not like to work?"

> I once lost a job and was able to start receiving unemployment benefits. These benefits turned out to be a double-edged sword; the money sure helped pay the bills, but it also allowed me to be too picky and maybe less aggressive in finding a job.
>
> When I had passed the one and a half year point without finding a job, I was starting to face the prejudice against the chronically unemployed. To break out of the rut, I had to actually change careers.

Many times employers will look at you with a skeptical eye if you are unemployed. They may think, "Why does this person not have a job?"

You will be questioned during an interview about each break in work on your resume. You need to be ready for these questions and prepare answers.

It is always easier to get a job when you already have a job. You are seen as someone who is working and you don't have that desperation when it comes to negotiating for a salary.

> I once lost a job and didn't have the luxury of going on unemployment. Within the week I had obtained three part-time jobs. When I went to my next full-time job interview, the interviewer was impressed that I was working and I got the job!

DOING SOMETHING

If you are out of work or you are working in a job that is not in your field, it is important that you continue to use your skills and maybe even improve your skills.

An employer wants to know what kind of passion you have for a job. It shows passion if you have been keeping up with your skills even though you are not working in your field.

How do you do it? Maybe you practice your skills by helping your neighbors in your field of expertise. Maybe, you take a short course to refine one of your skills.

> I was interviewing with Pan American World Airways and I hadn't had a flying job in several years. Of course, during the interview they asked if I had done any flying lately.
>
> I was able to tell them that although money had been very tight lately, I felt it was so important to keep up with my flying skills that I had visited the local airport and paid for several flight hours. They were impressed -- I got hired!

BE WORKING

I believe that it is so important for you to be working when you go looking for the job of your dreams. Not only does it give the right impression to your next employer, but it gives you confidence.

I never felt quite right when I was unemployed. Even the times when the company just went out of business, I had feelings of inadequacy. I always felt more confident once I was employed again. If you don't have a job, then go get something and you will feel better!

Chapter 12: Education

"Education is learning what you didn't even know you didn't know."

- Daniel J. Boorstin

SUDDENLY OUT OF WORK

The world has changed. No longer will people start at a job and stay in that job their whole careers. Unfortunately, I counseled so many people that never thought their job would end and therefore never upgraded their skills. Suddenly, they are out of work and out of touch with their field.

> The Information Technology (IT) field changes so fast that it is almost easy to fall behind. Fortunately, the college I work at offers seminars, courses, certificates, and degrees where someone in the IT field can upgrade their skills.

SKILLS UPGRADE

It is best to sit down with a counselor and discuss your options. What is right for a person depends on their skills and background. Here are some possible education upgrades that you can take:

- **Seminars** - Seminars or conferences are great ways to extend your knowledge in a new technology. Although there are usually some demonstrations, seminars usually don't offer a hands-on environment.

- **Courses** - Maybe you already have a higher level degree in your field and you want some hands-on practice in a new technology. A course that runs an entire semester is a great way to learn a new skill and you actually get to practice that skill.
- **Certificate** - If you are out of a job and you realize that you have fallen a little behind in your skills, a certificate program might be just the thing to show your passion for your field.
- **Degree** - Many people got into their field with no formal education and they are finding it impossible to move up in their company and realize it would be hard to find a new job if they had to. Starting a degree program at night might be the best strategy for these people.

NOT EVERYTHING

Education is not the right solution for everyone. I see so many students who don't fully take advantage of the classes they take. Don't waste your time and money unless you are ready to devote yourself totally in your learning process.

"Education is one of the few things a person is willing to pay for and not get."

- William Lowe Bryan

Chapter 13: Location - Dream to Move

" For the baby boomer generation, a home is now seen not as the cornerstone of advancement but a ball and chain, restricting their ability and their mobility to move and seek out a job at another location. "

- Mortimer Zuckerman

WHY MOVE?

Maybe you have decided that you want to stay in the small town that you grew up in. There is only one problem; this town has no jobs in your field.

Maybe there are jobs in your area, but they just aren't the best jobs. Looking in other areas might just be the best thing for you. In a tough market, you may need to go to where the jobs are.

> Most of my students like to stay in New Hampshire after they graduate which can be limiting, as there are many cities in the United States that have more people than New Hampshire.
>
> I remember one student that was determined to land a job in Boston. He peppered every company in Boston with his resume his last semester and was successful in getting a good job at about $15,000 more than his NH counterparts.

Have you ever seen the ads on TV for California or Hawaii and thought you might want to live there? Why not take a chance and get a job there?

You have to be a little careful and take a good look at the cost of living in an area. A $50,000 job in San Francisco might seem fantastic, but that might barely pay rent!

> I remember getting on a plane for Colorado to go to college -- I had never been in Colorado before. This started a trend in my life where I have been able to work in California, Mississippi, New Hampshire, Massachusetts and Texas. It was a little scary at times to move to a new place that I had never been, but in the end it was worth it!

I've seen people who wanted to change locations do it in two different ways. Each way has its benefits and detractions.

The first way is to look for a job long distance. The advantage is that you can keep the job you have until you find one where you want to live. The disadvantage is that some employers are reluctant to hire someone who is not already living locally.

The second way is to just pick up and move to where you want to be and look for work when you get there. I've always thought this was a courageous move, but many people have been successful doing it this way.

The bottom line is that your dream job might not be in your local area. Dream to move someplace else and open up your horizons!

Chapter 14: The Interview

- A wise person once said

"You never get a second chance to make a first impression."

THE INTERVIEW PROCESS

Picture this, a company receives 300 applications for their latest job posting. A secretary, using a skills list, makes the first pass through the resumes circling key skills on each. Then, according to some skills formula, 200 of these applicants are eliminated. Do you think your resume isn't important?

The hiring manager now reads all the remaining resumes and tells the secretary to set up the top ten for an interview. Of these ten, one declines, one shows up late, and two show up inappropriately dressed. This leaves six qualified people -- now the interview is what separates these applicants.

Of these six, one person hadn't bothered to research the company thoroughly, two had poor interview skills, and one showed no excitement for the job during the interview. In the end, only two gave themselves a chance for this job because of their great resume and interview skills.

HIRABLE TRAITS

What type of person does a company want to hire? This is not that hard of a question; think about your successful co-workers and what traits they all possess. Here is a list of traits that I look for when I hire a person:

Excitement - I want a person that can't wait to get to work in the morning. This is the number one trait that I look for. Many employers agree with me -- they always say that they can teach expertise, but they can't teach excitement.

Confidence - The days when you could lock an employee in the back room are over. Every employee in your company will at some time come in contact with your customers and when they do you want them to exude confidence. This confidence will spread to your customers.

Discipline - No matter what field you are in, it takes a lot of discipline to be successful. Events will go wrong and it takes discipline to focus on company goals when plans fall through. Great workers always strive to better themselves and that takes a lot of discipline.

Loyalty - Who wants an employee that talks badly about their current boss or co-workers? No one wants to hire someone who only thinks about themselves and who may leave the company at the first better offer. Modern day bosses realize that employees move on -- just don't give that impression during the interview.

Positive Mental Outlook - Are you the type of person who sees the glass half empty or half full? For salespeople, this is an essential trait; for everyone, this is an essential trait during the interview. People with positive attitudes always get the job done better than people with poor attitudes, and employers know this!

Expertise - Employers want competent workers. They don't expect you to know everything, but they expect you to know how to learn from your mistakes and grow into your job.

Notice that expertise is the last trait that I have listed. Usually, if you have obtained the interview, then you have the expertise needed for the job. Some job interviewers never ask any technical questions.

I know several companies that hire based on how well they feel a person will fit in with their team and not necessarily how expert this person is. They can always teach technical skills. Learning interpersonal skills is much harder.

PREPARATION

The interview actually starts many weeks before you show up to vie for your job. Since interviewing skills are so important, you should be spending some time every night answering interview questions out loud. Let me repeat myself here; interviewing is so important that you should be practicing every night.

Sometimes the greatest answer in your mind sounds pretty lame once you speak it. Don't just ask yourself the questions, get someone to ask you. Practice will make you more confident. If you are a poor speaker, then you should think about joining a group like Toastmasters International so that you can better yourself.

There are plenty of resources out there on the web with thousands of possible interview questions. Print as many different sets as you can and practice as much as possible. Videotape your answers and see where you need to improve.

> I remember the first time I substitute taught for a fifth-grade class. I was so nervous that I couldn't even introduce myself without my voice cracking. It makes no sense that a former Air Force aviator should be afraid of a bunch of 12 year olds, but I was afraid of the new situation.
>
> Guess what? The second time I substituted I wasn't nearly as nervous and by the time I had substituted a dozen times I had lost all my fear of standing up in front of a class.
>
> You do not want to be nervous during your interview. Practice, Practice, Practice!

COMPANY RESEARCH

Besides practicing your interview questions, you must research the company you will soon be interviewing with. You almost always get asked a last question which asks if you have any questions for the interviewer(s).

This is a great chance to show how excited you are about this opportunity by asking a question about the company that shows you cared enough to research the company. Remember, companies want to hire motivated people who are excited about their company, not necessarily the most qualified person for the position.

> One of my students visited an instructor that worked for me just before his interview. My instructor asked him what he knew about the company he was going to be interviewed at and he admitted that he knew relatively nothing. Together they researched the company on the Web and off he went for the interview.
>
> He got the job and the interviewer mentioned how impressed he was with the student's knowledge of his organization. He mentioned that many people he interviewed didn't even know what his organization did!

During your research, take the time to write down several questions about the company in a notebook that you should take to the interview. For instance, "I saw on your website that you merged with ABC company last year. Can you tell me how that came about and how it affected your employees?"

Again, interviewers are impressed with interviewees that care enough about the interview to research their organization. Besides, what if you found something disturbing about the company while you were researching? You could decide to decline the interview and save yourself a bunch of time or you could go to the interview for practice.

PROPER DRESS

From your company research, you can probably get a good idea of how to dress for the interview. I suggest that you always dress one level above what level everyone at the company wears on a daily basis.

If everyone wears jeans and a T-shirt, then you should show up in business casual. If everyone wears business casual, then you should show up in a nice suit.

I owned a real estate agency once and one Christmas, when sales had slowed way down, I thought I might work for UPS and make some extra money slinging boxes around during the holidays.

I showed up for an open interview in a coat and tie, ready with my resume. When I looked around, I knew something was definitely wrong. Somehow I had gotten into the Pirate job interview line -- everyone around me was wearing holey work pants and greasy sweatshirts.

When the time came for my interview, the young lady looked at my resume and then at me and said, "Mr. Laurie, have you ever had a job where you had to do anything physical?" I was in big trouble.

My initial thoughts were to stand up and body slam her to the ground, saying, "How's that for physical?" I didn't follow up on my thoughts, but maybe those actions would have gotten better results.

I was totally shocked and ended up mumbling some pathetic answer -- chock this job loss up to poor interviewing skills.

If I knew then what I know now, I probably would have said something like, "The physical aspects of this job will absolutely not be a problem for me. I was a collegiate athlete and I work out on a regular basis. But you don't want to hire me just because I can move more boxes than anyone else in line, you want to hire me because I have enough job experience so that I will show up every day on time and sober. You want to hire me because I will show up every day wearing the correct uniform with all the correct safety equipment. You want to hire me because I won't leave before the job is done even though my scheduled time is over. You want to hire me because I am an excellent worker!"

That answer probably would have worked a lot better, but I didn't know enough then to say it and I didn't get the job. I hope you can learn from this.

If you don't have the correct clothing, there are many places where you can get help. "Dress for Success" is a non-profit organization that provides interview suits, confidence boosts, and career development to low-income women in more than 75 cities worldwide. Many of my male students have been able to find suits at a reasonable price at Goodwill or the Salvation Army.

> I had one student show up at my office looking for an internship at the exact instant a company called looking for an intern. I put him on the phone and he made an interview appointment for the next hour. Unfortunately, though, he looked like he had just returned from a week-long fishing trip.
>
> He left my office in a hurry and went to the Salvation Army where he purchased a nice shirt, a pair of pants and a belt for nine dollars. He got the internship!

ON TIME BUT NOT TOO EARLY

The interview starts the minute you drive into the parking lot of the company where you are interviewing. If this company has security, then you have a great chance to make a good impression on the first employee of the company you want to work for. It never helps an interview if you are brought to the interview room in cuffs!

You definitely do not want to be late, but you don't want to be too early. If you have to take a weekend drive to make sure you know exactly where the company is, then do it. Try to arrive at the office you were told to go to 15 - 20 minutes early.

If you smoke, I would not smoke for at least two hours before you arrive and certainly not outside your car in the parking lot. Many times, the difference between two interviewees is very small; you don't want to give them any reason to choose the other candidate.

GREETING THE RECEPTIONIST

When you enter the office for your interview, be really nice to the receptionist. This can be hard sometimes as you may be very nervous, but be ready to make the effort. If the boss later asks the receptionist how she liked you and she gives you the thumbs down, then it doesn't really matter how well you interviewed -- many bosses have learned to trust the instincts of their receptionists or secretaries.

If you haven't done so already, try to get the names and contact information of the people who will interview you so that you will be ready to send thank you notes or e-mails after the interview. As you are waiting, take the time to organize your notes and practice in your mind how you will smile and greet everyone in the interview room. Don't forget to be pleasant to the receptionist.

When you are brought in for the interview, make sure you smile as you greet everyone. Women tend to naturally know how to do this. I've had male students whose faces might crack if they ever smiled. This is something that you can add to your interviewing practices -- practice smiling not only when you meet the interviewers, but when you answer each question.

POSTURE

When you sit down, make sure you sit erect -- no one wants to hire a slouch. Sit a little forward in the chair -- try to look eager. Arrange your notebook and pen in front of you (if there is a table) and place your hands in your lap.

When asked a question, make sure you look the interviewer directly in the eyes. It is better to pause to formulate your answer, when asked a question, then to just blurt out the first thing that comes to mind -- make sure you don't let your eyes wander while you think.

HOW TO ANSWER QUESTIONS

Eye Contact - Always look the interviewer straight in the eyes. If you let your eyes wander, then you will appear to be squirrelly -- no one wants to hire squirrelly people. I really have nothing against squirrels, but they just don't interview very well!

Pause For Effect - You don't want to rattle off your answers like a machine gun. It brings more emphasis to a subject if you pause for effect. Maybe you are answering a question about a work history gap on your resume, "You are probably wondering why I didn't work for almost 1 1/2 years starting in 2009." <pause here for effect> "My baby daughter Elaina Marie is the answer!"

Story - If you can work a personal story into the answer for a question then it helps to create a bond between you and the interviewer. The more the interviewer knows about your life, then the more connection he or she will feel towards you. The more connection he or she feels towards you, the more they will want you to join their team.

Solution - If you can share a story where you came up with a solution for a problem then all the better. Employers love employees that can own a problem and come up with their own solutions without having to rely on management. Here is your chance to portray yourself as the hero or heroine!

QUESTION CATEGORIES

The Softball - Interviewers always try to give you an easy first question, something to relax you. If you are not ready for this type of question then the interview might go downhill from there. Examples of this easy softball type question are:

- "Tell us about yourself?"
- "Why do you want this job?"
- "Why would you be good for this job?"
- "What would your co-workers say about you?"

If you are ready for these questions, then you should be shouting "Yeah" in your mind when you get one. Way before you go to an interview, you should prepare a list of bullets of important points you want to bring up in the interview. These questions are a great way to check them off your list. These bullets should be designed specifically to bring out the traits mentioned earlier in this chapter.

First impressions are so very important; you need to knock this question, out of the ball park. If you stumble on this first question then your chances for employment at this company are not good.

What might a great answer to this first question look like?

"My name is Susan Forsyth and I am so thrilled to be interviewing here today. I have been watching your company for many months now and I was so excited to see a position posted that I was extremely qualified for."

"Customer service has always been a passion of mine and my hard work was rewarded last year when I was selected as Front Desk Employee of the Year. I can't wait to apply my skills to this position."

"I have been at my current position for three years and truly love the company that I work for. If offered this chance for improvement, I would sadly leave my company family."

"I love hiking and I love meeting people!"

Notice how in this answer, Susan has shown almost all of the hirable traits. If she delivered her answer in a clear confident voice, then she might have hit all six traits in her first answer.

The Trap - Many times you will be asked a question to see if you will say something negative about a co-worker or a boss. Make sure you never do this! If you say negative things about co-workers and bosses, your prospective employer may worry you will speak negatively about their company..

- What bugs you the most about your co-workers?
- What didn't you like about your last supervisor's management style?
- Can you think of a co-worker that really didn't have the company's best interest at heart?
- What trait did you least like about your boss?

> Many times, I ask my classes this question, "Have any of you ever had a lousy boss?" You would be amazed at the answers I get! Remove this type of thinking from your mind -- even the worst bosses can teach you valuable things and you should never talk about them.

The answer to these questions should always be the same. You should think long and hard, but fail to come up with any examples. Again, if you talk badly about your former boss and co-workers, what will you do about your future ones?

The Unanswerable - These are questions that an employer doesn't expect you to know the answer to. They are asked to see how well you perform under stress.

- Why did they put fuzz on a tennis ball?
- Who was the 33rd signer of the Declaration of Independence?
- What is the speed of sound?
- How many gallons of water are in the Indian Ocean?

Don't guess! Admit that you don't know the answer but you know of many resources to find the answer. Expand on how you might find the answer.

"I really don't have a clue on how to answer that question, but I would start by "Googling" it. I also have some text books at home on that

141

subject that I could check and I have some really smart friends. I'm sure I could find that answer quickly!"

The Management Theory - You will get asked this type of question many different ways. They all are aimed at getting your idea of what constitutes good management.

- If you were boss, how would you manage?
- How does a good boss act?
- What kind of management style produces the best results?
- What does a successful manager look like?

Your answer should always emphasize that good leadership/management is an equal mix between people skills and task orientation. You can answer this question something like this:

"I really admire a manager who takes an interest in his or her employees, stands up for them, praises them, but who also can encourage a desire to work hard and complete the task at hand."

or

"I've always liked a boss who pushed me to be the best I can be, but also always considered my best interests."

The Illegal Question - Even though employers have been warned and have taken courses to prevent it, they still ask illegal questions or questions bordering on being illegal. These questions many times deal with age, family responsibilities and lifestyle. The following are examples of these types of questions:

- How are you coming with your child care?
- Where were you born?
- When were you born?
- What nationality are you?
- Do you rent or own a home?
- Does your spouse work?

This is not a great situation. You have to decide whether you really want to work for someone who asks illegal questions. If you do, you can answer an illegal question with indignation or humor.

"I've been working so hard lately, that, frankly, I don't even remember where I live!"

or

"That's a really strange question. Why would you ask me something like that?"

The Experience Question - This is probably the most important question you will answer during an interview.

Don't be modest; highlight your experiences in a strong confident voice. Experience questions might take this form:

- Tell me about your last (current) position.
- What successes have you had?
- Give me an example where you solved a customer problem.
- Describe a typical day at work.
- What makes you stand out among your peers?

It is important to give answers to these questions that relate to the job you are applying for. This will take some research about the company and some forethought before you go to the interview. Here is a possible answer:

"One day in my front counter job at McDonalds, a highly inebriated man came in who wanted to cause some problems. I was able to calm him down, get a phone number, and call a friend of his to come get him. I believe my ability to think quickly on my feet and my ability to connect with people will serve me well in ACME company."

Closed-ended Questions - These are questions in which an interviewer is looking for a specific piece of information. Although you can sometimes answer these questions in single words, try to give a full sentence answer. These questions might look like:

- Is that correct?

144

- How many years did you work in that position?
- Is that the first time you experienced that problem?
- Does this clarify your confusion about our security policy?
- What are your salary expectations?

One worded answers make you seem stiff and uninviting. If you were asked how many people you supervised, you might say:

"In my time at Spacely Space Sprockets, I was given more and more responsibility until I was supervising 13 employees."

Hypothetical Questions - These are questions asked by employers to assess your critical thinking and problem solving abilities. They may look like the following:

- What would you do if you found out a fellow employee was stealing from your company?
- What would you do if you felt your boss was totally wrong in what he/she was asking you to do?
- What if your boss asked you to do something you thought was unethical?
- How would you resolve conflict in a group situation?
- If you got on an elevator and everybody was sitting down, what would you do?

Since the employer is trying to gauge your problem solving skills, it is certainly acceptable to ask questions to gather more information, and to think out loud while listing possible solutions before coming up with a final answer.

You better have answers for some of these questions before you show up. If asked what you would do if you knew your boss was making the wrong decision, you might say:

"I would get my boss alone and explain distinctly why I thought he was coming to the wrong decision. I would be as forceful as I could be, but in the end I would realize my boss might be making the decision on information that I was not privy to and I would support my boss in public."

Leading Questions - Many times these questions lead to an answer. Don't fall into the trap of answering the question the way you think the interviewer wants you to answer it; if you disagree, then voice your objections. The following are examples of leading questions:

- Not all students belong in college, do they?
- You really didn't get along with your last boss, did you?
- You must be a good communicator, aren't you?
- A good manager cares about his people. What will you bring to this team?

Never be led to giving an answer that is not what you believe or is a negative answer. Take your time and thoroughly think these questions through before answering. An answer to the first question might be:

"I believe that all students who are ready for the rigors of college belong in college."

Multi-Barreled Questions - These are questions in which the interviewer asks more than one question in a question. This is where a notebook comes in handy, and you can write down each question to make sure you give all answers. Don't be afraid to ask the interviewer to repeat or rephrase the question. A Multi-barreled question might look like the following:

- What was the last professional development that you did, where did you complete it, and why did you choose that particular development?
- Was there ever a time when you were stressed at work and how did you handle it?
- What do you think about our latest product? Do you think our advertisement campaign was effective? If so, how?
- Have you ever been fired from a job? If so, why?

Don't get confused because of the multiple questions. An interviewer might conceal certain trap questions in a multi-barreled question in hopes to trip you up. Just take your time and answer each question separately, according to the question type.

Behavioral Questions - These are questions aimed at how you reacted to certain situations in the past and are some of the hardest questions to answer cold. They also present the greatest opportunity to really nail the interview by giving specific examples as to how you handled these situations.

You must do your research and think about how to answer hundreds of these types of questions before you ever interview. Behavioral type questions might look like these:

- Tell of a certain time where you had to comply with a certain policy you didn't like.
- Give an example where you used logic to solve a problem.
- Describe a situation where your co-workers would have described you as being a leader.
- Have you ever made a mistake and how did you resolve it?

These questions are great ways to create a bond between you and the interviewer. You do this by including a personal story to answer the question. An answer to the policy question might be:

"Someone had to work on Christmas day in our company. Since I was single, I volunteered to work the morning shift so that other family employees could be with their kids on Christmas morning."

The Fishing Trip - Interviewers are always looking to find out your weaknesses. It doesn't work to come right out and ask something like, "Are you lazy?" -- but they might start fishing by asking something like:

- "What is your greatest weakness?"
- "What is your greatest strength?"
- "How would your boss describe your work habits?"
- "What motivates you?"

If you are not ready for these questions, if you have not prepared answers for these questions, then you might not come across well. Remember, many times the interviewers are not looking for what you say, but at how you say it!

> I once had an interviewee answer that his greatest weakness was procrastination. With this answer, he immediately moved to the bottom of the stack of potential employees. He learned from that interview and the next time we interviewed him, we hired him.

What can you say is your greatest weakness?

"I am so driven to complete a project that I have to sometimes force myself to leave work and relax."

or ...

"My desire for perfection sometimes makes me spend too much time on a project. I have learned that meeting deadlines is more important most times than having the perfect document."

or ...

"I am so focused sometimes that I have trained myself to listen to what a customer is asking rather than trying to solve their problem before they are finished speaking."

Do these answers sound contrived? You bet they do, but they are much better than something you might come up with on the fly! Interviewers are impressed with someone that has taken the time to think of answers to possible interview questions.

ACTION WORDS

Study any list of action words that people recommend for resumes. Practice using these words during interviews. Wouldn't it sound more powerful to say, "I prioritized my options before I solved the problem," rather than to say, "I picked the best option and finished the problem."

SALARY EXPECTATIONS

You will commonly be asked salary questions during an interview. Prevailing logic says that the first person that mentions a number loses. If you answer with a number too high then you risk alienating the interviewer. If you choose a number too low, you just took a pay cut.

One of the best ways to answer this is to turn the question around on the interviewer, "I'm not looking for a higher salary than what is normally offered. What salary range does your company offer for this position?"

Another way to answer this question is to have done salary research before you show up for the interview and say, "My research says that employees in this position generally get between $17 and $21 per hour (or $34,000 - $42,000). I would be comfortable in that range."

LAST THOUGHTS

The worst thing that could possibly happen to you is to lose your dream job because someone who had better qualifications than you interviewed better than you did! Of course, you'd rather hear this from an interviewer, "We want to hire you. Your qualifications weren't as good as some of the other candidates, but it seemed you will fit better with our company."

Practice!

Practice!

Practice!

Chapter 15: Answering Objections

" Don't Handle Objections Like Snakes."

- Charles H. Green

FIRST INTERVIEW

In high school, there was a new McDonalds's restaurant in town and it was the best job to get for a 14 year old at that time. I dressed up, went for the interview, and ran into the age-old "catch 22" question, "What job experience do you have?" How could I get a job that asks that question when I had never had a job?

If I had known then what I know now, I would have answered that question differently. I might have said, "I don't have any experience cooking hamburgers, but I have enough experience to know that you want someone who will show up on time wearing the correct uniform. I may not know how to clean a Fryolator, but I have enough experience to know that there will be times when I have to work an extra shift if someone doesn't show up. I may not know every facet of running a cash register, but I have enough experience to know that I have to treat every customer with respect and dignity."

I can almost guarantee that if a 14 year old answers a question like that they will get hired. I didn't answer that way and I didn't get hired.

Note: I didn't learn how to answer that question right away. It took me many years of experience to realize how to answer that. I hope you will learn how to answer those objections from this book.

One of the best ways to handle an objection during an interview is to answer the objection before it comes up. Sit down and take a long hard look at yourself and come up with a list of objections an employer might have. Come up with answers for these questions and add them to the list of answers you want brought out during any interview.

Sometimes a company will be bigoted towards you, and there is nothing you can do to be hired by them. If you have answered all their objections and they still won't hire you, then tip your hat to them and move on to the next better job. You probably don't want to work for them anyway.

Here are some common objections and how you might handle them. Being prepared during an interview is the second best thing you can do; the first is being able to show excitement for the job.

worked as a cashier at a supermarket, how could you answer a question emphasizing teamwork?

You might say, "As a cashier, I had to coordinate with my manager and my bagger every day to provide the customer with the best service possible."

Customer service is a great skill to always emphasize!

TOO MANY RECENT JOBS

Although companies don't expect you to stay with them for 30 years anymore, they do expect loyalty from you. If they see you as being a job jumper, then that is not a good thing. So, how would you answer the question of having too many jobs in a short period of time?

You might say something like this, "I left ABC Company because it was a small company and there was no place to move up. I realized soon after starting at XYZ Company that my skill sets did not match their expectations and I left and started working at LMC Corporation. I am now ready to move on and am really excited about the opportunities at your company."

TOO MUCH EXPERIENCE

If you are questioned about having too much experience for a job, then there is probably an underlying question that hasn't been voiced. They may be thinking you are too old for this job or they may be thinking you won't be as motivated in a job that you have done before.

You must answer the underlying questions before this objection comes up. So, how do you answer the age objection?

You might say something like this, "I am very excited about this job and I can't wait to bring my experience and drive to this position. I have learned the ins and outs of this industry and I can't wait to bring my ideas and dreams to this company. I know the pitfalls of this position and I won't be making the mistakes many new hires do. Can you imagine how fast I can get up to speed in this position and be operating at 100% within days, not weeks!"

So, how do you let the interviewer know you are motivated about the job?

You might say something like, "You might wonder why I applied for this job that I have done many times before. I love doing this job; I'm very good at doing this job, and I plan to do this job for many years. Give me a chance to continue my career with your company and you will see the energy and drive I bring to this job!"

Remember, showing excitement about a job is very important. If you go into an interview and can't show excitement for that job, then you will never get that job no matter how you answer the objections.

> Note: Sometimes you really have too much experience for a job and the person hiring you is worried that you are better qualified for their job than they are. In this case, they will never hire you.
>
> I once interviewed for front desk manager at a major hotel chain. It was obvious that I had more experience and more education than the manager I interviewed with -- he was afraid to hire me in case I wanted his job one day. There was nothing I could have done in that interview.

CRIMINAL RECORD

Everybody makes mistakes and employers are willing to hire people that have turned their lives around. However, you will never get hired in some industries with certain criminal records. For instance, if you got convicted of a child sexual crime, then you will never get hired as a teacher.

I believe that honesty is the best policy. I would write up a description of what you did, when you did it, and what you have done to turn your life around. I would then include this memo with any job application.

This will certainly limit the places that will hire you. I guess I would rather eliminate these places than be fired a month after starting the job when your employers find out about your record.

The larger the company, the more likely they are to do a background check on you. You won't lose anything by turning in this memo.

At some point, your only option will be to start working at a small company without revealing your background. If you work for them long enough, then you will have a track record that will help overcome your criminal record objections.

TEAMWORK

If a company thinks that you don't have teamwork skills, then you haven't done your job during the interview. Teamwork is so important in so many jobs that you should always strive to emphasize your team working skills in every answer. If you

> I worked for three companies that went bankrupt in a row. When I applied for my next job, it looked like I might have been job jumping. I made sure that I explained in my cover letter why I had changed jobs so many times.

NOT A GOOD FIT

This is usually the killer for a job. If the interviewer has decided that you are not a good fit, then you will never get the job. You might ask, "What type of person would be a good fit for your company?" This won't help you get the job, but it might be valuable information on how you were perceived during the interview. If you were perceived negatively, then you can use this to improve yourself for the next job.

Remember, never burn your bridges. Thank the interviewer for their time and leave on a good note.

LACK OF A PARTICULAR SKILL

An interviewer might never mention this, but you might perceive this from the interviewer's body language. If you see poor body language in your interviewer, then it is best to isolate this objection by saying something like, "I see that you are concerned about my lack of skill A. Frankly, if I were in your place, so would I. If I could show you that I could do skill A, would that affect my candidacy?"

If they say "Yes," then you can approach your next statement in two different ways. You could explain your experience with skill A, but what if you really don't have that skill?

You could say something like, "I really don't have any experience with skill A, but I remember a time in my last job when they needed me to learn skill B and I was able to learn that skill in a few short weeks and become an expert within the first year. I am sure that I could learn skill A very fast."

TOO MUCH EXPERIENCE

If you are questioned about having too much experience for a job, then there is probably an underlying question that hasn't been voiced. They may be thinking you are too old for this job or they may be thinking you won't be as motivated in a job that you have done before.

You must answer the underlying questions before this objection comes up. So, how do you answer the age objection?

You might say something like this, "I am very excited about this job and I can't wait to bring my experience and drive to this position. I have learned the ins and outs of this industry and I can't wait to bring my ideas and dreams to this company. I know the pitfalls of this position and I won't be making the mistakes many new hires do. Can you imagine how fast I can get up to speed in this position and be operating at 100% within days, not weeks!"

So, how do you let the interviewer know you are motivated about the job?

You might say something like, "You might wonder why I applied for this job that I have done many times before. I love doing this job; I'm very good at doing this job, and I plan to do this job for many years. Give me a chance to continue my career with your company and you will see the energy and drive I bring to this job!"

Remember, showing excitement about a job is very important. If you go into an interview and can't show excitement for that job, then you will never get that job no matter how you answer the objections.

> Note: Sometimes you really have too much experience for a job and the person hiring you is worried that you are better qualified for their job than they are. In this case, they will never hire you.
>
> I once interviewed for front desk manager at a major hotel chain. It was obvious that I had more experience and more education than the manager I interviewed with -- he was afraid to hire me in case I wanted his job one day. There was nothing I could have done in that interview.

CRIMINAL RECORD

Everybody makes mistakes and employers are willing to hire people that have turned their lives around. However, you will never get hired in some industries with certain criminal records. For instance, if you got convicted of a child sexual crime, then you will never get hired as a teacher.

I believe that honesty is the best policy. I would write up a description of what you did, when you did it, and what you have done to turn your life around. I would then include this memo with any job application.

This will certainly limit the places that will hire you. I guess I would rather eliminate these places than be fired a month after starting the job when your employers find out about your record.

The larger the company, the more likely they are to do a background check on you. You won't lose anything by turning in this memo.

At some point, your only option will be to start working at a small company without revealing your background. If you work for them long enough, then you will have a track record that will help overcome your criminal record objections.

TEAMWORK

If a company thinks that you don't have teamwork skills, then you haven't done your job during the interview. Teamwork is so important in so many jobs that you should always strive to emphasize your team working skills in every answer. If you worked as a cashier at a supermarket, how could you answer a question emphasizing teamwork?

You might say, "As a cashier, I had to coordinate with my manager and my bagger every day to provide the customer with the best service possible."

Customer service is a great skill to always emphasize!

TOO MANY RECENT JOBS

Although companies don't expect you to stay with them for 30 years anymore, they do expect loyalty from you. If they see you as being a job jumper, then that is not a good thing. So, how would you answer the question of having too many jobs in a short period of time?

You might say something like this, "I left ABC Company because it was a small company and there was no place to move up. I realized soon after starting at XYZ Company that my skill sets did not match their expectations and I left and started working at LMC Corporation. I am now ready to move on and am really excited about the opportunities at your company."

> I worked for three companies that went bankrupt in a row. When I applied for my next job, it looked like I might have been job jumping. I made sure that I explained in my cover letter why I had changed jobs so many times.

NOT A GOOD FIT

This is usually the killer for a job. If the interviewer has decided that you are not a good fit, then you will never get the job. You might ask, "What type of person would be a good fit for your company?" This won't help you get the job, but it might be valuable information on how you were perceived during the interview. If you were perceived negatively, then you can use this to improve yourself for the next job.

Remember, never burn your bridges. Thank the interviewer for their time and leave on a good note.

LACK OF A PARTICULAR SKILL

An interviewer might never mention this, but you might perceive this from the interviewer's body language. If you see poor body language in your interviewer, then it is best to isolate this objection by saying something like, "I see that you are concerned about my lack of skill A. Frankly, if I were in your place, so would I. If I could show you that I could do skill A, would that affect my candidacy?"

If they say "Yes," then you can approach your next statement in two different ways. You could explain your experience with skill A, but what if you really don't have that skill?

You could say something like, "I really don't have any experience with skill A, but I remember a time in my last job when they needed me to learn skill B and I was able to learn that skill in a few short weeks and become an expert within the first year. I am sure that I could learn skill A very fast."

Chapter 16: Salary Isn't Everything

"I'm the first to admit this whole salary thing is getting out of control. In the final analysis, it's still about the work."

- Jim Carrey

JOB BENEFITS

There is no salary in the world that makes having to go to a lousy job every day worth it. The corollary to this is that a job with a lower than industry salary might be fantastic, depending on the benefits.

What are some of the extra perks that might make a lower paying job worth it:

- **Autonomy** - Many jobs give you the flexibility to choose your own hours and choose your own direction with little or no supervision as long as you produce.

> Being a teacher is one of the greatest jobs on earth. There is a lot of hard work, but you have almost total autonomy in how you teach. If you try something new and it doesn't work, you can always tweak it the next semester or can it and try something else.

- **Time Off** - There are some jobs where it takes an act of God to get a certain day off and there are other jobs where getting time off is very flexible. Find out what the policies for this are before you consider a job.

- **Medical Benefits** - This can be very important when you have a young family. A great health care plan is a huge benefit for any job.
- **Flexible Hours** - Some jobs will fit the hours you need to work to best fit your lifestyle. Maybe you need to leave early every day to pick up your kids but are allowed to put in hours at night after they have gone to bed.
- **Commute** - When I changed jobs and my commute tripled from four minutes to 12 minutes I didn't mind. When I moved again and my commute tripled again I started longing for my original four minute commute. Those who have 15 second commutes from their kitchen to their home office really have a great benefit.

When I was a pilot for Pan Am, I commuted from New Hampshire to New York City. When the weather was good, it was an easy drive down to Boston and a quick shuttle flight to JFK. When the weather was bad, it was a nightmare and many times I would have to get to New York City a day early!

- **Parking** - Does your work provide parking or do you have to spend 20 minutes every day searching for space? Find out what the cost of parking is before you accept any job -- in a city environment it can be very expensive.

- **Increment Pay** - In many jobs an annual review determines whether you get an increment raise. Sometimes, companies have no flexibility when offering a starting pay, but you can negotiate for a six month review.

- **Education Benefits** - Many employers will pay the cost of one or two higher education courses per semester as long as these courses are working towards a degree in your field.

- **Retirement Benefits** - The days of working for a company all your life and receiving a retirement are almost over. Matching payments into a 401(k) retirement savings account is the standard and should be looked at carefully.

- **Military Leave** - If you are in the National Guard or the Reserves, you must find out how a prospective company handles it if and when you are called to active duty.

- **Child Care** - Does your company have actual child care on premises or do they have a child care subsidy? This can be a very great benefit.

The bottom line is that salary isn't everything. The worst possible decision you can ever make is to take one job over another because a salary that is a few thousand dollars more, just to find out you are very unhappy in that job.

> I was once trying to get a new job and I kept interviewing at this one place as they offered an average higher salary. Luckily, I never got hired there, as I heard many horror stories about working conditions there.
>
> I ended up taking a position at a lower salary at a place that had fantastic working conditions. In the end, I moved up, matched the salary I wanted and was a lot happier!

" Find a job you like and you add five days to every week."

- H. Jackson Brown, Jr.

Chapter 17: Following Up

"Success comes from taking the initiative and following up...
persisting... eloquently expressing the depth of your love. What
simple action could you take today to produce a new momentum
toward success in your life?"

- Anthony Robbins

Following-up is often the difference between success and failure.

> I once met a fetching young woman. About a week later, I finally got enough confidence to ask her out on a date. I called and she told me to call back in 20 minutes as she was busy cooking dinner.
>
> Was she really busy or just trying to get rid of me? She did answer the phone when I called back. If I had not followed up, I would not have had the chance to date and eventually marry the most wonderful woman.

SYSTEM

Come up with some sort of a system to remind yourself to follow up. When you visit a company that might be a good prospect and you get the name and phone number of the hiring manager, log your follow-up call in your system so that you don't forget.

I like to log these follow-up calls into Microsoft Outlook. If the person isn't there, it is very easy to move the appointment to another day. If you don't want to use an electronic system, then a simple day scheduler or calendar works well. The key is making the appointment to do the follow-up.

THANK YOU NOTES

If you get to meet with someone or you actually get to interview with someone, it really makes a great impression if you follow up with a thank you note. People really appreciate these notes; it adds to their impressions of you as being on the ball, and if nothing else it keeps your name in their minds.

You must be very meticulous when you visit or interview at a company and get correct contact information. In an interview situation, it is possible to get the contact information for everybody interviewing you before you actually walk into the interview.

I believe an e-mail is a perfectly acceptable form for a thank you note. If you want to stand out, a handwritten card can be very effective.

PERSISTENCE

Business people are very busy and you have to be very persistent sometimes in your follow-up.

> My friend Jack tells the story about submitting the application for his current job. By following up he found that his application never made it to the required person. His application was actually lost three different times.
>
> He eventually hand-delivered his application to the correct person. If he had not followed up, he might never have known why he didn't get the job!

It is almost an art form to navigate the phone systems of certain companies. Even when you get the correct phone number, you can be stonewalled by a secretary or administrative assistant.

If I need to talk to someone with authority at a company, but have a hard time getting through to them, I have used this little trick with great success. Call during the day and get the phone number to the person's office who you want to contact. Call back just after closing time. I have found that once the secretaries have left for the day, many times a boss can't resist answering a blinking phone.

LONG-TERM FOLLOW-UP

You never know when you might lose your job. Companies go out of business suddenly and people lose jobs through no fault of their own.

The list of contacts you compiled during your job search is a valuable list to keep updated while in your job. If you keep this list updated, if you happen to lose your job or you plan to move on, you already will have a great place to start for your job search.

APPENDIX A: Cover Letter Examples

REFRIGERATION TECHNICIAN

This cover letter was designed for a refrigeration technician who is looking to be employed in the same field where he has several years of experience. Notice that his cover letter includes a referral, talked about excitement for the new company and listed specific skills pertinent to the job.

123 My Street
Any Town, NH 03301
603 555-1234

August 17, 2011

Mr. Bill Freeze
ACME Refrigeration
225 Elm Street
Manchester, NH 03101

Dear Mr. Freeze:

Bill Dobbs suggested I contact you concerning the Refrigeration Technician position available at ACME Refrigeration. I am inspired by ACME's dedication to green technologies and can't wait to join such a progressive company.

I provide a level of experience in refrigeration installation and maintenance. I believe I am a great fit for your company because of my:

- New England HVAC certification
- 4 years refrigeration installation
- silver soldering expertise
- Associates of Science degree

My resume is enclosed for your evaluation. I will contact you during the week of August 30th to schedule a time to further discuss my qualifications for the Refrigeration Technician position. Thank you for your time and consideration.

Sincerely,

Robert Jones

GENERIC IT INTERNSHIP

This cover letter was designed to be generic for applicants looking for an IT internship. You would use this cover letter when you are out following the aerobic job search (intern search) approach from Chapter 6. Of course, if you know the companies you plan on visiting on a particular day, you should spend the time to customize each cover letter.

88 Melody Lane
Hopkinton, NH 03229
603 555-4321

October 21, 2011

IT Hiring Manager:

I am currently a second year student at NHTI - Concord's Community College where I have been focusing on Networking. I have been fascinated by computers ever since I touched my first Pentium II when I was eight years old.

I am searching for the perfect company for my second semester internship where I can broaden my education with some practical application of the skills I have learned in class.

I am currently enrolled in my third semester of CISCO and I recently passed my CCENT Certification. I have a strong desire to be a Network Administrator and I hope that your company will help me start in the right direction by offering me an internship.

Although the bulk of the internship should be accomplished in the second semester of this school year, I am available to start immediately.

My resume is enclosed for your evaluation. I hope we can further discuss my qualifications for an internship position with your company. Thank you for your time and consideration.

Sincerely,

Andrew Smith

PROGRAM MANAGER

This cover letter was designed for a program manager position in the telecommunication field. Notice that this cover letter highlights a specific achievement in the telecommunication field.

44 My Street
Beverly, MA 01915
617 555-1234

February 15, 2011

Mr. Bob Applebee, President
Teracycle Telecommunications
123 Broad Street
Amherst, MA 12345

Dear Mr. Applebee:

Please consider my extensive qualifications, as summarized on the attached resume, for a position of Project Manager with your company. The experience I have gained in the Telecommunication field since I obtained my MBA makes me extremely qualified for this position.

In my previous position, I supervised a 5.4 million dollar 900 MHz Mesh technology conversion in a major US company. My basic understanding of financial metrics was essential to the implementation of this wireless technology.

In addition, I have enjoyed a reputation for being an extremely dedicated employee. I am excited about the opportunity to work for such an innovative company as Teracycle. I would appreciate the opportunity to interview with you. Thank you for your consideration.

Sincerely,

Barbara Olsen

ON-LINE

This cover letter is designed to upload to different job sites. It therefore must be generic. Also, you should probably store it in an unformatted version so that it can be copied and pasted onto any website.

12 New Balch Street
Beverly, MA 01915
617 555-4321

March 15, 2011

To Whom It May Concern:

Please consider my extensive qualifications in
the Telecommunication field.   The experience I
have gained in the Telecommunication field
since I obtained my MBA makes me extremely
qualified for this position.

In my previous position, I increased on-air
advertising 23% in my first two years.   The
creation of several ad campaigns was
instrumental for this increase.

In addition, I have enjoyed a reputation for
being an extremely loyal employee.   I am
excited about the opportunity to work for the
fair and balanced Fox News.   I would appreciate
the opportunity to interview with you. Thank
you for your consideration.

Sincerely,

Tom Hanson

FIRST TIME JOB

This cover letter was designed for a young person who has little or no experience and may have never held a job.

44 My Street
Beverly, MA 01915
617 555-1234

February 15, 2011

Ms. Susan Lance, Manager
Old Navy
123 Commercial Way
Amherst, MA 12345

Dear Ms. Lance:

I am very excited about your open position for salesperson. I have always had a healthy interest in clothes and I can't wait to help customers find exactly what they need.

Although I have never formally worked for a company, I am no stranger to customer service. My many years of babysitting has refined my ability to please my customers.

Please note on my resume my perfect attendance award in school. I excel at always showing up to work on time, ready to give my best. I can't wait for the opportunity to interview with you.

Sincerely,

Suzy Newbie

APPENDIX B: Resume Examples

ENTRY LEVEL IT

This resume was designed for a student who just graduated with a two year IT Associates of Science degree looking to get a job as an Application Developer. Notice that there are many key words in the top third of the resume separated between Technical Skills and Course Work. This student should be prepared to answer any questions from the Skills section.

Thomas Anderson

Bunk 4,
Nebuchadnezzar, Matrix, 00001   neo@yahoo.com
Cell: 603 555-1224

TECHNICAL SKILLS

- ASP.NET
- C#
- VB.NET
- SQL

- CSS
- Threading
- Javascript
- Java

- HTML
- AJAX
- Sockets
- MS SQL

WEB SITES
HTTP://WWW.MYWEBSITE.COM

COURSE WORK

- XML
- Cryptography
- Gimp
- PC Hardware and Software
- Polymorphism

- Classes
- Inheritance
- Java
- Windows Server
- Web Services

- Networking
- Finite Math
- ADO.NET
- User Controls

WORK EXPERIENCE

Cashier (*2007 – 2008*)   **Deli Clerk** (*2008 – Present*)
MARKET BASKET, Concord, NH

Selected to train new employees after only six months on the job. Instituted labor saving ideas that energized fellow employees to provide superior customer service. Identified as an exemplary cashier within one year of employment.

- Trained new employees
- Provided superior customer service
- Awarded "employee of the month"

Camp Counselor (*Summers 2002 – 2006*)
CAMP BELKNAP, Laketown, NH

Created and deployed a comprehensive plan to educate campers in basic computer skills and computer ethics. Entrusted with the care and safety of young children during their daily activities.

- Responsible for the safety of sixteen 7-year-old children
- Taught Introduction to Computers classes
- Yearly recertified in First Aid and CPR

Hobbies – Ultimate Fighting, Rock Climbing

189

FIRST-TIME JOB

This resume was designed for a young person who has never really held a paying job. The old "catch 22" about how can you ever get experience when many jobs require experience is always true for first-time job seekers. Can you imagine how Suzy would stand out if she attached this resume to the application of the local fast-food restaurant!

Suzy Newbie

123 My Street,
My Town, NH 03301
Cell: 603 555-1224

first@yahoo.com

SKILLS

Responsibility

Selected as Junior High Biology Lab Assistant. Completed the Lab Safety course in record time and performed lab duties flawlessly.

- Helped teacher set up labs
- Helped order needed supplies
- Cleaned up lab after use

Healthy

Awarded perfect attendance award for all eight grades attended.

Dependable

Understands that the job is not done just because the clock says it is done. Willing to work overtime to make sure all tasks are completed.

Flexibility

Available to work varied hours when not in school. Has solid transportation.

Determination

Balanced schoolwork and babysitting without letting either interfere with the performance of the other.

- Received High Honors throughout Junior High School
- Selected as top Biology student two years running
- Babysat over 20 hours every week

Communication Skills

Created the first lab manual used to train future Biology lab assistants. Placed second in the annual Fourth of July speech contest at local VFW.

WORK EXPERIENCE

Baby Sitting *(2007– Present)*
Neighborhood

Asked to provide after school care for my three younger siblings for the past four years. Established as weekend babysitter of choice in neighborhood.

- Completed First Aid babysitter's training
- Developed science projects for younger kids
- Saved brother from choking on small toy

191

ON-LINE

If you upload a resume to a popular on-line job site you risk that the company receiving or looking at your resume won't have compatible software to read your resume and cover letter. There is also a chance that an on-line job site may not be able to index your resume correctly, thus limiting the searching companies can do for you. The following resume was created as a straight text file that should be able to be read by anybody. You can use this resume to copy and paste to these sites.

Bill Salesman
123 Anywhere St, Lancaster, NH 03584
cell: 617 555-1212
SALES REPRESENTATIVE

Professional Strengths:
Client Training
Sales Growth
Client Increases
Media Relations

Experience:

Boston WXRM Radio, Boston, MA
Lead Sales Representative

Managed team of six sales representatives.
Created classic brand recognition for station.
Grew on air advertising 23% in two years.
Launched extremely successful "Taste of Boston"
campaign.

WGIR New Hampshire's NEWS Radio, Manchester, NH
Account Executive

Top producer 15 out of first 24 months.
Created over 100 new accounts.
Developed new weekend programming for client

Education:

MBA, Harvard Business School
Boston, MA

TEACHER WITH FANCY QUOTES

If you want to emphasize some of the great things said about you in your references, then this might be the resume for you. The only problem here is that if you need to keep your resume to one page, then you lose valuable page real estate by using a column of quotes. The quotes do make this resume stand out!

Wanna B. A. Teacher
8 School Road, Concord, NH 03301
603 555-1212
wbateacher@gmail.com

TEACHING EXPERIENCE/RELATED EXPERIENCE

Red Barn Elementary School, Concord, NH
Intern Fourth Grade Teacher
Implemented lesson plans according to the Everyday math curriculum. Utilized Fountas and Pinnell curriculum for literacy development. Designed and implemented a three-week curriculum on simple machines. Designed and adhered to a unit-end summative assessment rubric for simple machines.

Peterson Elementary School, Penacook, NH
Intern Second Grade Teacher
Implemented lesson plans according to the Everyday math curriculum. Attended methodologies in literacy Developmental Reading Assessment training with Educational Consultant Kelly Brothers. Conducted several DIBELS Benchmark Assessments. Created lesson plans based on the Open Court program. Designed and implemented a curriculum on the study of germs. Adhered to a variety of Responsive Classroom techniques on a daily basis. Participated in faculty meetings, in-service days and parent/teacher conferences. Developed close personal relationships with each of my students.

Peterson Elementary School, Penacook, NH
Learning and Adjustment Assistant
Academic and social issues. Worked closely with other professionals in the Learning and Adjustment program and classroom teachers to intervene when a student was in crisis, diffuse situations and maintain a safe environment for all.

92.5 The River WXRV, Haverhill, MA
Promotions Department Assistant
Promotions Team member at an independent, solar powered and locally owned radio station. Responsible for overseeing and attending important promotional events and to act as an ambassador for the company. Supervise and record interviews and meet-and-greets with listeners, musicians and major record label associates in the River Music Hall and at venues throughout the greater Boston area.

SERVICE TECHNICIAN

Here is a blue-collar resume. The technical skills and qualifications are very important just like in any resume where you want to pass the first resume screening process. Like many industries, this one lends itself to the aerobic approach of job hunting, and having a professional resume is a great head start.

Robert Technician

123 My Street
My Town, NH 03301   technician@yahoo.com   Cell: 603 555-1224

SUMMARY OF QUALIFICATIONS

- CDL-A driver's license with passenger endorsement
- Qualified high voltage test technician (100Kv and below)
- Qualified ANSI 92.2 lift inspector
- Spotless driving record

TECHNICAL SKILLS

- Diagnosis and repair of electro-mechanical-hydraulic systems used in aerial devices and equipment
- Crane troubleshooting, service & repair
- Operator; truck mounted hydraulic cranes
- Customer service/repair representative working remotely from central service center

PROFESSIONAL EXPERIENCE

Mobile Service Technician

Comcast Technologies, Manchester, NH

- Traveled daily to customer sites in Maine, New Hampshire, Vermont, and Massachusetts to diagnose and repair hydraulic lift trucks and equipment
- Addressed customer concerns independently with regard to their maintenance needs
- Repaired auxiliary truck systems to include: DC power inverters, transmission power take offs, and related electrical interfaces with Allison transmissions
- Trained others in skills required of a mobile service technician

Manufacturing Engineer

GE AIRCRAFT ENGINES, Hooksett, NH

- Responsible for process support
- Quality plans for twelve turning centers producing ten different rotating parts
- Design of lathe fixtures, special carbide tooling and tool holders
- Process documentation, and statistical analysis of process data
- Redesigned inventory of carbide inserts resulting in significant savings. Processed control engineer evaluating discrepant hardware

197

INDEX

U

UNEMPLOYED, 9, 111
USAJOBS.com, 92

W

WEIGHT, 7, 39

THE LOSING ATTITUDE

FOR DIETERS

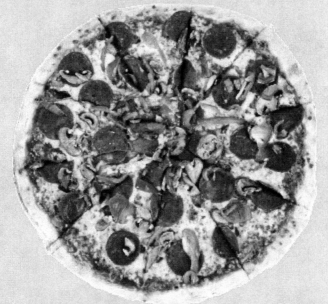

Supercharge Any Diet through Healthier Lifestyle Choices

PROFESSOR TOM LAURIE

CPSIA information can be obtained at www.ICGtesting.com
Printed in the USA
LVOW091459250412

279141LV00014B/63/P